A

DEATH
Lived

• • • ● ● ● • •

MARTHA CALIHAN, MD

Dedication:
Dedicated to Charles,
my teacher, my love…..always

Prologue

. . . ● ● ● ● . . .

There was snow on the ground that Wednesday morning as
we left for the emergency room in the dark; by the time we
returned home, the forsythia was in bloom.

Charles had awakened with a numb, cool, and then a painful right
foot. Although I knew that, medically, this could have been any one of a
number of problems, I was worried. With Charles' history of heart disease
and peripheral vascular disease, I was worried that he might be experiencing an occlusion of blood flow to his leg, similar to the process of a heart
attack, when there is a blockage of blood flow to the heart. What it was
specifically, though, I didn't know. What we also didn't know was that this
was the start of the final chapter of his life.

The other thing I didn't know when entering this process of his final
illness was that it would be a deeply sacred and profound experience, and
ultimately, a gift far beyond anything I could have imagined. Since I had
first met Charles when I was sixteen years old, he had always been the
teacher; first in school and then later, in life. In the end, it turned out that
he kept right on teaching, both through his act of dying and beyond. I
deeply believe that one of Charles' purposes in this life was to teach as
many of us as would listen, how to die.

Medical science and highly trained personnel, most of whom were my colleagues and our friends, would do the very best that could be done for Charles, to save his life.

Of that I had no doubt. But our medicine ultimately would fail, as it must when someone's physical life is, in fact, ending. We, and those we love, will each die one day, and for Charles, we were coming to the end of the path.

But we were also at the head of the path on another journey—one that raises questions for us all. Is death the end, or is there an aspect of us that leaves the body at death and lives on? Most of the science and medical world says there is not. Faith and the experience of so many says there is.

Can we know? If so, how?

This other journey was one that would allow me to witness the most sacred experience of my life as both wife and physician, sometimes together and sometimes separately, sometimes smoothly and sometimes in conflict, the one role with the other. This journey required me to hold my dual realities simultaneously: those of a physician and a wife. It was a journey during which I was about to walk a path with my husband that would span both my worlds and where I would walk along the narrow ridge that separated the two.

I am a conventionally trained, Board Certified physician, and as such, I have been present at many deaths. I know what happens—or I thought I knew. The heart stops, respirations stop and the person is declared dead. But the truth is that I had always wondered about death, and what really happened at the moment a person dies. What was the difference between being alive and being dead? What, beyond the fact that the heart no longer beats and the lungs no longer breathe, changes? What happens? I was certain there was more to it than the simple change in the physiology; the biology. But what that "more" was, I didn't know.

And where in the process was the spiritual aspect? I had been taught about death from the Catholic perspective as a child but I sensed that there was something more there, something seemed missing, something that I didn't comprehend.

Now I do know that there is more to death than biology. The science of death, as I was taught in medical school, is very clear. Prior to experiencing what I'm about to tell you, my questions about death were all hypothetical. But now my experience was different, and challenging, because what I witnessed was very different from what I thought I knew. Was I right? Or was I "needing" to see this because I was a sleep deprived woman who was losing her husband? Was I just making myself feel better? Is that what other people would think? Was I crazy?

When I was young, and growing up, death for me had been a thing; death meant gone. It was more of a noun than a verb. It was not a process, an experience, and there was never much thought about the context other than to ponder the meaning of "forever."

I remember being told that my grandfather had died; I have the picture clearly in my head of my mother telling me that she was leaving to go to his funeral; what it meant to me was that my birthday had to be postponed....

It wasn't until I began my medical work and career that death became an organic process for me, and thus the questions.

I began to question not only what actually happened at the moment of death, but also what it meant, and what followed it. When I watched, I knew that there was more—much more—than just being gone. With witnessing and reflection, death became a process; more verb than noun.

And what about the process of dying itself? Is it something to fight at all costs?

What is reasonable and makes sense to an individual going through that process? Are there options? How does one navigate this universal but most challenging experience?

The medical world, as I knew all too well, tends to view death as a failure. Most physicians are not fully comfortable with the concept of letting go when someone is dying; of encouraging or even allowing, a different path. As a culture, we are death-adverse. But we can do better. This I know, both as wife and physician. And the experience, although a painful one, can be rich and poignant.

Charles' death, to me, was profound and mystical. I know now that death is, or can be, that for all of us.

And perhaps I now understand that having navigated this most difficult and painful experience, I was given the gift of understanding—the gift of a knowing that will be with me the rest of my days.

Chapter One

· · ◦ ● ◉ ● ◦ · ·

On March 17, 2010, after having awakened with the cold, numb foot, Charles and I arrived at the Loudoun Hospital Emergency Room and the process started--off to interventional radiology for Doppler studies which showed no pulse or blood flow in his right leg. The decision was made to have the interventional radiologist attempt to open it up and start thrombolytic (clot busting) therapy. We had to move quickly, because a limb without adequate blood flow is in real jeopardy; the tissue will die if the blood flow can not be restored in time. And Charles was in a lot of pain from the blockage that was the presumed source of the lack of blood flow. The pain was most likely being caused by a blood clot, and that had to be remedied soon if his toes and his foot were to be saved.

There was a problem, however. Surgical back up was necessary in case the blood vessel was damaged during the procedure, necessitating surgical intervention, and our friend and my colleague, Dr. McDow, the vascular surgeon, was out of town, and this meant that perhaps he would need to be transferred to a tertiary hospital, 20 miles away. We really didn't want to do that. Charles had been there before for surgeries and procedures; it had not been a great experience and he was simply, more comfortable being "home" at Loudoun.

Over the years, Charles had endured many medical procedures, most of which had been related to his longstanding cardiovascular disease, and he had experienced heart attacks, heart surgery, carotid artery surgery and repair of an abdominal aneurysm. He had suffered his first heat attack in his early 40s, and he was certainly considered "high risk." But we knew and trusted our team at Loudoun and this was where we wanted to be, if at all possible.

Thankfully, another surgeon agreed, very graciously, to cover the procedure and would be available if anything surgical was needed. Although he wasn't officially on call and covering for Dr. McDow, he too was a colleague and agreed to help us out by being available should the need arise. The radiology team was able to place a catheter into the artery that was blocked and start the medication to dissolve the clot. The plan was to leave the catheter in place and to continue the thrombolysis (clot buster) and blood thinners for 24 hours, and then the following day, Thursday, bring him back to the interventional radiology lab to repeat the procedure to see what progress had been made. He was admitted to the ICU so that the blood thinners could be continued under close observation, and we began the waiting process.

So far, this was feeling oddly routine: as a physician, I was well trained to encounter a problem, analyze it and then determine the necessary intervention. So many times, I had discussed cases with these same physicians; the language was understood; there was shared knowledge. These were my colleagues, my friends.

But this was my husband, and we were discussing his blocked arteries and treating his leg, whose viability was threatened. In that moment, I wasn't so much physician as wife … and mother.

As soon as he was in getting the dopplers, I was able to get in touch with our son, Conor, who happened already to be in the hospital at his job as the administrator of the anesthesia group and he quickly joined us downstairs. Conor was Charles' third son, and our only child. At 24, he was off on his own, but the three of us maintained a special closeness that was to grow even stronger in the coming year. Conor is strong— physically and in presence—with a generous and kind heart. He was confident and tender, loving and full of life, with red hair and an infectious laugh that always made Charles smile when he saw him.

So it was no surprise that Charles' eyes lit up at the sight of him. But Conor and I exchanged a glance that we both understood without needing to speak the words; the situation with the leg was a problem and we were, potentially, in trouble here. Conor's work in the anesthesia world, coupled with having grown up with me actively practicing medicine had given him a strong understanding of medicine, and he understood that the arteries blocked by blood clots are not always able to be opened up and kept open. Too often, these patients ultimately end up needing amputation of the affected part. And we knew, too, that with Charles' cardiovascular history, the other arteries were likely not healthy; this could be just the tip of the iceberg.

Conor, then 24 years old, had grown up with Charles being intermittently, and increasingly, un-well. Charles' medical history was full of cardiovascular disease as well as two bouts of colon cancer for which he had had surgery and chemotherapy. The colon surgery had been complicated by a small heart attack, one of the many he had suffered over the years. So, illness in his father was part of Conor's reality, and had been since he was a small child. They were incredibly close. It was hard to watch my son, now a grown young man, having to deal with yet another instance of his father being not well. It seemed that as time went on, and the medical events kept occurring, that Conor had to step into the role of caretaker more often. And he always seemed to keep a watchful eye on me as well; it was bittersweet.

Charles, who was 71 years old, had a particularly severe variant of cardiovascular disease, which had manifested in his heart, his aorta, his carotid arteries and his legs.

Several years earlier, he had undergone multiple procedures and finally a bypass operation to keep the blood flowing to his legs. The fact that we were back here again, with evidence of progression, was ominous. This type of cardiovascular disease often does progress, but his course seemed to be progressing more rapidly than might be expected. Though I was encouraged by, and grateful for, the success of the radiology team that morning in opening the blockage, the physician in me knew the precariousness of the situation. I knew that this progression of his disease and the rapid rate at which it was occurring was a poor prognostic sign; it wasn't likely that it would stop or even slow down at this point. And I couldn't help wondering, *where would this end up?* Each medical event, it seemed, had taken its toll. And yet, each time, I waited anxiously to get him back home and get back in the rhythm of our lives; where we would re-adjust and re-calibrate to whatever the new situation demanded. That had always been our goal, to get back home and be together. And so far, we had always been able to do that.

Charles and I had been married for close to thirty years, and had been together for many more. I had known him for over half my life, and we had the great fortune to have a marriage and relationship in which we were more than marriage partners; we were each other's best friends. I absolutely adored him and he, me. We each knew that we were in this together, for the duration, and we were grateful each time we were able to return home and resume our lives, whatever changes that required.

As had become our habit during all of his recent hospital stays, I stayed with Charles; we were fortunate to be in "my" hospital where we were known and even more importantly, understood. This was the hospital in which I had practiced medicine for the last twenty years, a small enough facility where we mostly all knew each other and to which Charles had been admitted on many prior occasions. So, despite still being a hospital, this was basically as comfortable as it could be for us. In turn, I think that the ICU nurses would agree that my presence with him actually made everything easier. For one thing, he was less apt to get confused, and the entire experience was less stressful.

Charles had a history of getting confused in the hospital, and although mild confusion in a hospital setting, with the altered routines and constant interruptions is common, his confusion was sometimes more than mild, and on one occasion, had had a true case of ICU psychosis, probably drug induced. When I was with him, I was usually able to help minimize his confusion. It wasn't that my presence was a guarantee that he wouldn't get confused, because he absolutely did, but it helped that I usually was able to settle him down fairly quickly if he seemed to be heading in that direction.

Normally, Charles was one of the most well-informed and intelligent people I had ever known. With what seemed to be a photographic memory, he remembered everything. Seeing him get confused and not be clear on these occasions in the hospital was incredibly challenging and difficult on a personal level. And perhaps not unexpectedly, on those occasions, anger would often accompany the confusion, making the experience even more painful and difficult for us both. I know that the anger was most likely a result of him feeling the loss of control when he got confused and his frustration, nonetheless, it was, frankly, deeply disturbing to witness, and something which I tried hard to help him avoid.

For the next two and a half days, we remained in the ICU with the thrombolytic medication being infused into the blocked artery in his right leg and with the intravenous blood thinners running as well. Each morning, we returned to the Interventional Radiology lab for another arteriogram to assess the progress. Each day there was less clot and more flow; his foot was warm and had a pulse. The threat of losing the foot and/or the leg was diminishing and the prospects of a good recovery increased. Charles remained alert, positive and upbeat through all this; he never complained and once the blood started flowing there was less pain.

Conor spent time with us each day—checking in before work, between meetings and in the evenings. There were lots of calls with friend and family—Sean and Colin, Charles' two older sons, my mother and siblings, colleagues and Charles' and my friends. In a fairly small town and a close medical community, word travelled fast. Whereas I spoke with many of my colleagues, Conor often ended up speaking with our friends, and certainly with his brothers and sometimes other family members when I was tending to Charles.

Though I would answer their questions about how he was doing and tried to be reassuring, I found that somewhere inside I had some doubts and I worried that others could detect these doubts in my voice and my answers.

I recall one particular phone call I had with my sister, Sara, who was a social worker and lived in Boston. She understood people, and was quick to pick up on my uncertainty and inability to project complete confidence that Charles would, in fact, be OK. She had helped me navigate many of his medical episodes through the years, and she and Charles had a very close relationship.

"So how is he?" she asked.

"OK, I think; they seem to have the situation under control…." I responded, to which she answered, "and how are you?"

This was typical of her; keenly aware of how hard this was for me.

I hesitated, and tried to be strong in answering "OK, I think…" and only then, let myself feel my fear that maybe he wasn't OK, and that maybe they wouldn't be successful. "Actually, I am not sure; somehow this feels different to me" I found myself admitting. "I don't really know why I am not more confident about the outcome, perhaps it's my intuition?"

My intuition has always felt strong to me, and it is something I feel is important to acknowledge and honor. I have learned, over the course of my life, to listen to those seemingly random bits of "knowing" or sense that come to me, and to pay attention.

Why couldn't I be more confident and re-assuring about the outcome, I wondered.

And what did it mean that I couldn't? There was nothing objective to cause me such doubt, I told myself. But my intuition felt differently.

On Friday morning, Charles returned yet again, to the Interventional Radiology lab; this time the radiologist, Dr. Joseph, was sufficiently satisfied that he deemed the clot busting procedure complete. He would leave the catheter with the clot busting medicine in Charles' leg for another two or so hours, check the blood to make sure the blood thinners were working, and then the catheter could be pulled. This was great news. For the past two and a half days, he had needed to be flat on his back and keeping his legs straight as there were catheters in the arteries. Having the catheters pulled would create a brand-new freedom; he would soon be able to sit up, and also eat. During the previous couple of days, with the persistent threat of needing an emergent surgical intervention, he had only had liquids; Tuesday night's dinner became an increasingly distant memory and he had become hungrier...

Back in the ICU, Charles was given some pain medicine; three days flat on his back was beginning to bother him. Everything was quiet. His blood pressure, though, was quite high despite the pain meds—in the 200/100 range, going as high as 210/110. This was worrisome; even for someone with known high blood pressure, these were high readings. I kept hoping that some rest and decreasing the pain would help bring that down. He tried to rest as Conor and I sat by his bed.

After a couple of hours, the radiology tech came upstairs and checked his blood. He was deemed "in range" and the catheter was pulled from his groin. That left a large puncture wound in a very large artery in a man who had had massive doses of blood thinners and clot "busting" medication. The tech dutifully held his fist on the groin site for a full twenty minutes, applying sufficient pressure to stop the bleeding.

When all seemed quiet. I decided to go home so I could tend to the dog and get a change of clothes; Conor would stay with his father while he had his lunch, and then he would go back to work when I returned.

Driving back home to Leesburg was disorienting to me. Though I had been in the hospital with Charles for only the past 72 hours, it felt like an eternity. I had lost any connection with what was happening in the world, having lived in the insulated bubble of the hospital, with the entire focus on Charles' leg. I had almost forgotten a world beyond ours in the hospital existed. To be back out in a world that was unaware of the drama that was playing out in our lives was difficult. It made me realize how often people we encounter are consumed in their own private dramas and how little we might know about what is going on in their lives.

I got home and took our dog, Orla, out for a short walk. It takes three to four minutes to walk down our driveway and back but in that time, I had missed three calls from Conor. He called again before I could return his call and said, "You might want to come back. Dad is bleeding, and his blood pressure is dropping." He was clearly worried.

"Tell me what is happening," I replied. "Who is there with him?"

"A bunch of nurses, they have called for Dr McDow. Come fast, please!" Twice more on my drive back to the hospital, he called.

"How close are you?"

"His blood pressure is only about 70." Conor sounded scared; I panicked. I hadn't felt this scared in all the times that Charles had been at critical points in the past and he had been in some tight jams over the years—several heart attacks, colon cancer twice, urgent surgery for a large abdominal aneurysm. This time felt distinctly different and all I knew was that I was frightened.

Luck let me find a parking place near the Emergency Room; I entered the hospital and began to run. Running through the hospital to the ICU felt interminable. I arrived in the unit to find the ICU room filled with people and equipment; Conor stood in the far corner of the room, his eyes wide. There were nurses, a respiratory therapy technician, Dr Mendiguren, the ICU physician, and the charge nurse there with her phone making calls and the "crash cart" filled with the drugs and equipment they use in an emergency.

Charles lay flat on his back, in Trendelenburg—meaning that the head of the bed was lowered. Patients are placed in this position when their blood pressures are dangerously low, in an attempt to prevent it from getting any lower. A couple of nurses were starting additional IVs to give him fluid. Charles was drowsy but conscious, seeming to drift in and out.

I tried my best to reassure Conor, but my words were not convincing; we both knew that we just had to wait this one out and see where it went; they were doing what needed to be done to resuscitate him.

Equipment and people filled the room—people I had known and worked with and some I had never met. They were starting additional IVs to help support his blood pressure, which was by then about 60 and not recovering; his heart rate was slowing as well. There was blood everywhere. He had bled from the puncture wound in the groin, and had lost a lot of blood.

I started medical school in 1978, after working as a tech in the operating room for two years with the open-heart surgery team at Georgetown University Hospital. I had seen, participated in, and eventually run many "codes" in my career. (A "code" is the response to a cardiac arrest or some other similarly severe and critical situation. Most of the time, the code team ends up putting the patient on a respirator and performing CPR to try to restart the heart when it has stopped.)

In our case, Charles' heart hadn't stopped, and he was still awake and breathing; but his heart rate was dropping, his blood pressure remained dangerously low and he was beginning to lose consciousness—fading in and out a bit. This was scary, literally watching the man I loved fading away from me. And there was nothing for me to do but stand there and watch...

So, yes, I was familiar with "codes." However, to witness a code being run on Charles, the man I loved, the other half of my whole, was overwhelming. It was also a beautiful thing to watch; a well-run code is like a well-choreographed dance with an entire team of people coming together to do what they are trained to do to save someone's life ... I saw my colleagues and friends, and some I didn't know, doing the dance for my Charles....

It is unusual to allow family members to remain present in the room during a code or even a critical situation, but neither Conor nor I were about to leave and no one tried to force us to, for which I was grateful. In the end, for me, it was easier to know what had happened than to wonder. In our case, we saw firsthand, the lengths people went to save his life, and the effort made in doing so.

Over the course of my career, I have experienced a number of occasions in which there has been a role change—either I was seeing a colleague as a patient, or I was being seen as a patient by a colleague, and many times where I was present as the spouse when one of my colleagues was taking care of Charles. It can be a difficult switch to make, and I have always been impressed with those who do it well. I have had the good fortune to see it done well in quite a few instances and one of those times was on this day, when I watched friends and colleagues take over and manage a most challenging situation, one in which Charles could have died.

There in front of me was Dr. Medniguren. "Mendi" as he is called, was the intensivist who was present in the ICU running the Code. I knew him well, having shared many critical patients over the years. His expertise put him in the most dire of situations, yet he was fun loving and warm, always talking about his daughter and family trips. On this day, as always, he was cool, calm, competent and kind. His intensity, from his dark hair and eyes, to his muscular body, belied a gentleness and presence that reassured even in the tensest of situations, I was relieved and grateful he was there.

He did what had to be done and managed to keep me informed as to what was going on and to allow me the space to be the wife, not a physician, as I needed and wanted.

And then there was Russ, Dr McDow, our beloved surgeon and friend, back in town after a few days away. A tall, Southern man with a glint in his eye, whom I had never seen in anything other than scrubs. I saw him in the door of the ICU and felt instant relief. He had been in the OR when the call went out that Charles was in trouble. He hadn't been able to get up to the unit right away, but when he did arrive, he was cool and appeared calm. Russ had already operated on Charles several times over the years, twice for his colon cancer, several times for his legs and for his carotid artery. Charles and I had complete confidence in him; he was one of the best surgeons I had ever known. He was a gentle and soulful man, and a dear friend.

Russ stood in the doorway and surveyed the room, the monitors, and Charles, and made note of everything that was happening. I was increasingly frantic, but watched as he quietly was convinced that the bleeding had stopped. He finally looked at me and silently mouthed the words, "He's not going to bleed to death while I am here." At that point, the full realization of the situation began to sink in. It was as if the burden of it all had been handed over to Russ, and I had a deep internal, intuitive knowing that in fact, Charles would be all right.

Slowly, with the addition of IV medication to keep his blood pressure high enough and his heart rate up, he began to improve. He received a blood transfusion and things started to settle down. The members of the code team started to dissipate, the high tension began to evaporate.

By that point, Charles was exhausted. During the bleed, a device had been placed on the femoral artery to prevent any further bleeding; it's called a fem-stop—a round, disc-like device attached to straps which go around the patient and can be tightened to put pressure on the groin where the incision had been. No one felt that he was stable enough to remove the device or clean him up after the bleed, it was elected to let him just lay there for a few hours and try to clean him up later.

There lay Charles, covered in blood. And there I stood, next to him, touching his hand, my fingers wrapped in his. I saw him with the eyes of both wife and doctor, terribly worried and enormously relieved.

Eventually, Conor left to return to work, and I think that Charles dozed off. I settled into the chair next to his bed—a position I would occupy many more times in the months to come.

During the next few hours and through the night, Charles received blood, his pressures were watched and his blood was tested repeatedly to see how much blood had been lost. The night nurse and I eventually were able to wash the old dried blood off and get him off the bloody sheets; the fem-stop was removed and all was quiet. Still tired from all the day's events, Charles was nonetheless intermittently awake and reached out to take my hand, saying "I love you." My heart felt as if it would burst as I responded, "Yes, I love you too." Did he know how close he had come? I wasn't sure, and didn't feel that was the time to talk it over. There would be time in the days that followed, as he rested and we got ready to go home. I, however, couldn't get it out of my mind.

As night fell, I lay in the reclining chair next to the ICU bed, where Charles lay hooked up to the monitors and the IVs. Rest would be minimal at best, as even nights in the ICU are not quiet. The commotion outside the room continued throughout the night. The nurses were tending to critically ill patients, monitors went off, the phones rang, people talked. Nighttime in a hospital is a world unto its own; it is night for the patients, but not for the staff. There is an entire shift of clinical people who show up each night and do the work of taking care of the people who need it. And neither illness, injury, birth nor death occur by the clock. Which is why in medical school and residency, our training includes working day and night, often without breaks. To witness and participate in the life and death situations that occur in a hospital, one needs to be there. You can't just read about it or hear about it in the morning to learn and understand. Working at night was hard on the body as a student and a resident, but really is irreplaceable as a training experience.

Compared to the daytime routine, that night in the ICU, things had slowed down and quieted a bit, and I was able to replay the day's events over in my mind. I relived my sense of fear, of panic, which was now mixed with my sense of deep gratitude for the team of people who had come together and saved Charles. They had saved his life! It was hard to acknowledge to myself those words, yet they were true and my relief was enormous. I felt a sense of pride in my colleagues, and in the medical technology that can be brought to bear. I really did realize too, how close we'd come to disaster.

Maybe that was why I also felt something else. In the back of my mind was an uneasiness, a feeling that in the greater sense all was not well. For a moment, I chided myself. Was I just being "Irish," as we call it in my family—looking on the dark side of things and leaning into the worst possibilities? Or was I really feeling a foreboding that this time was different? Or had we simply been through too many medical episodes and I was feeling that sooner or later, our luck would run out? Was my intuition really telling me that something was different? And was this my intuition or my medical knowledge that I was sensing? Did it matter which part of me, my head or my heart, was trying to be heard?

I decided that, in fact, this time it did feel different, for whatever reason, and I felt that I needed to listen to that inner voice, to that caution, and to pay attention. I didn't necessarily think there was anything to do, simply that I needed to be *aware*.

Chapter Two

. . . .

A s I lay there next to him in the ICU, contemplating both what had happened and what my intuition was sensing, I realized that I definitely felt tension between the part of me that was Charles' wife and the part that was a physician. I wanted to integrate these into a single entity, but I was finding that difficult. I found myself on unsure footing. I wasn't sure, either as a doctor or as a wife, if Charles' condition really was that bad or if this had just been a bad bout and he would, in fact, recover.

As a doctor, I knew that if the medical situation got worse, there were plenty of interventions that could be done. Another clot in the leg could be dealt with. A hemorrhage could be stopped again. His blood pressure could be treated. That should have been reassuring. And on some level, it was. But in my work with patients, I had begun to wonder about the wisdom of never-ending interventions and on a number of occasions, had even wondered out loud about the performance of endless "medical miracles" to keep people alive. Those occasions were different, however; they were theoretical discussions. Now, very suddenly, this was personal, this was *my husband*.

Here was the dilemma. If his condition did worsen, what would be the right thing to do? In an acute medical crisis, there are interventions that can help avert a potential disaster, and we were already on this path with Charles. We had always opted for interventions for his various medical conditions over the years—heart procedures, surgery and chemo for colon cancer, surgery for an aneurysm, etc. But sometimes, people get to the point where they opt to stop choosing more procedures, and opt for less, not more, intervention. Surely, I thought, we were not at a point where things looked so bad for Charles that we had to start making decisions about care, but why was I feeling this inside me? Clearly, we would do everything we could to remedy this situation. Deep inside, however, I was feeling some angst.

I wondered, *how did people in challenging and sometimes ambiguous situations know what to do?* So often in an acute medical crisis, a person's prognosis isn't immediately obvious, and can change as the situation changes. How do patients and families make decisions about treatment choices, particularly when the situation can be fluid and changing? Typically, there is a problem, then a complication and another problem and so it continues. What started out as a situation with a reasonable course of action to correct it suddenly becomes an enormous, complicated situation with challenges that hadn't been anticipated. It can be hard to make important life altering decisions "on the fly." So of course, people often don't know what to do, to ask, to choose. It's like being on a moving sidewalk, only a medical one. Once you get on, it can be hard to get off it, or even to know how to decide when to get off. And in our medical culture, there seems to be much more enthusiasm for getting on it than helping people get off it if the process isn't yielding the results that had been hoped for. We, the medical professionals, aren't always as skilled in helping patients and families in these difficult discussions as we are in treating the issues. I had the sense that we didn't know where this round would end and that it could take us to a place we didn't want to be. But I didn't know if I was thinking and reacting as a physician or as his wife. And didn't know if it mattered.

I decided that the best thing for me, and for us, at the moment, was to be mindful of what I was feeling and to try to hold these dual realities—wife and doctor—simultaneously, to allow both to be part of what I was experiencing and feeling. And to be open to what would happen and try to make the right choices at that time.

While that set of questions was circling in my head, another set also started to creep in. I slowly found myself thinking more about death and, in the larger sense, what that actually meant.

As with most people, I had always wondered about death, not only what constitutes the moment when the spark of life in the physical body ceases and what that's like, but also what happens to us after we die. I had never been able to believe that it was a simple scientific fact—that the heart stops and you are dead. Gone. Out like a candle. I always felt that it was more than that, but what that "more" was, I didn't know.

These are not thoughts you necessarily want to have at three or four in the morning. They're unsettling. It bothered me that I was lying there next to my husband, wondering about death when he had just had such a close call. But it struck me as not an unreasonable thing to be thinking about either, and—this close to disaster—I couldn't get the questions out of my head.

One thing helped. I knew that I would talk this over with Charles when he was stronger and recovered; we always had these sorts of conversations together. There wasn't much, it seemed, that we didn't talk about and I imagined this would be no different. In so many ways, Charles was always the teacher. He seemed to have wisdom and insight into life's mysteries. Many times, over the years we had talked about death; I was eager to have the conversation again.

Before we could get to that talk, though, we were again thrust back into crisis mode.

Chapter Three

· · ● · ● ● ● · · ·

Early the next morning, Charles developed chest pain which required nitroglycerine and morphine to alleviate. His blood pressure started dropping again, and he was seen urgently by the cardiologist on call, as clearly, something was wrong—the question was what? The concern was that perhaps the blood loss had compromised his heart and he was having another heart attack.

Charles had his first heart attack before we were married when he was only 40, and this fact was always in the background of our life together. He was fine after that for several years, but the fact of it was never completely removed. His family history was fraught with cardiovascular disease and slowly, his own health issues increased to the point where his health was no longer just an addendum, rather it was a main player in our lives.

The cardiologist made the decision to transfer Charles to Fairfax, the tertiary hospital, for urgent cardiac catheterization. I was concerned about the transfer because the cardiac cath procedure could lead to more intervention and I wanted to make sure that Charles was comfortable proceeding with a procedure whose outcome could mean open-heart surgery. That outcome is always a risk of a cardiac cath—either because of the findings or possible complications. A blockage might be found that would require a stent or surgery, the risk of perforating the artery and needing emergent surgery was a distant but real possibility.

When we discussed the transfer and the procedure, Charles' response was simply, "Okay." Knowing this could be big, though, I forced the further conversation about what he would allow. In my mind, there would be no point in having the cath if he wouldn't agree to heart surgery, should that be deemed necessary.

The cardiologist on call for the weekend spoke with us and filled in details about the procedure and the possible outcomes. In the end, Charles said, "Yes, I will agree to open heart surgery if that is what's needed." I was watching him closely. Although physically uncomfortable, he was lucid and coherent, and he seemed to understand everything that was being explained. He didn't look particularly scared. He had been down this road before. That having been settled, the arrangements were made for the transfer, and because of his instability, the helicopter was called to fly him the 25 miles to Fairfax Hospital.

As a physician, there had been many times over the years I had waited for the chopper to arrive at our hospital in Loudoun, usually with a very critical patient who needed to be transferred; there had always been a sense of relief to me that the team was there to get the patient to the next level of care, and relief that the treatment a patient desperately needed was available. Standing in the ICU and watching the chopper come down out of the sky, knowing it was coming for my Charles, was overwhelming to me. I was scared, relieved, sad and anxious all together. It felt surreal in part; although deep down inside I knew how serious this was and that it was, in fact, very real.

Once again, I called Conor to fill him on what was happening and he got to the hospital in about 10 minutes. Once he was in the room with us and the decision to transfer had been made, he was back on the phone with his brothers, updating them.

As the transport team entered the room, Charles was calm and didn't resist going; he was still having some pain but finally was medicated enough that it was mostly relieved. In a moment, he was placed on the tiny helicopter stretcher, belted and off they went. He was given headphones to protect his ears from the noise of the flight.

I had reached out and called my close friend, Susan Patch, who had just arrived from Richmond, and asked her to stop by our house to bring me some things that I would need at Fairfax. She arrived in the ICU just as they were preparing to wheel Charles out of the room towards the helicopter. Susan—tall, blonde, dressed in shorts, a tee shirt and a hat that made her look, as she said, like a 12-year-old boy—made Charles smile, and he looked at her and said, "love you." We kissed and said our goodbyes, I was grateful that he was smiling as he was wheeled out to the waiting chopper.

Knowing that we would not be able to see Charles at Fairfax until after his procedure and knowing that it would take them a total of 9 minutes to get there, we stood in the window of his ICU room, which looked out over the helipad, and watched. After several minutes, the door from the ER opened and they wheeled him out towards the waiting chopper; loaded him in and slowly pulled up off the ground, dipped a bit, turned and headed to Fairfax.

Conor and I waited a long time before the Fairfax team told us that Charles' cardiac catheterization was done and that we could see him. The doctor had gone straight into the next procedure so there were only bits and pieces of information, but it became clear that they hadn't found anything new or different; no action had to be taken. Charles would stay in ICU that night and the doctors would reassess him in the morning. He slowly woke up, and the three of us spent some time together. He was no longer having pain, and in general, things seemed pretty good. Eventually, Conor left to go home and I stayed with Charles for the night.

The next morning, an intern came in on early rounds and said brightly, "I want to see how you are doing after your heart attack." Charles looked a bit shocked; I was as well. This was the first anyone had told us about a heart attack. I knew it had to have been small, because the intern was telling us that the cardiac enzymes they use to measure the extent of heart muscle damage hadn't spiked very high. But for me, it was not just a medical evaluation, it was confirmation of the seriousness of what had occurred the day before during the bleed. He had lost enough blood to cause a heart attack.

"The enzymes have peaked," the intern was saying, "and you're stable. Your doctor has made arrangements to transfer you to the telemetry unit." The telemetry unit, often referred to as the "step-down" unit, is where patients go after they are stable enough to be out of Intensive Care but where they can still be monitored. "They will be moving you there as soon as there is a bed available."

Suddenly, ahead of me, I saw an entirely new and different landscape. We would again be dealing with the recovery from a heart attack, not just the blocked leg and the procedure to open that up. I knew that we would be looking at a much longer and slower recovery, but I also knew that we could do this; we had done it before.

Later that morning, when the cardiologist visited, he announced, "There is not much on the cardiac cath that was different from your condition before. Do you want to see your husband's films, Dr. Calihan?" Walking down to the cath lab, the doctor added, "You really need to take him home and just exercise him. He'll be fine."

I wanted to scream. This was not, in my opinion, helpful advice. It seemed to me that he had no understanding of what had transpired and why Charles had needed the cath. Perhaps it was just a routine procedure to him, but he didn't seem to be paying attention to the context at all. Hadn't he read any of the notes that came with Charles?

Didn't he understand that it was severe claudication (pain from a lack of blood flow) that had started this process? That Charles had just undergone a 3-day procedure to re-establish blood flow to the leg and that he had just had a heart attack from the blood loss when he bled? It seemed unlikely that significant exercise was going to be on the horizon for a while. I was disappointed by how out of touch this man was and by how fragmented the care seemed to be. I was too stunned to respond.

Back in Charles' room, the doctor pronounced, "You're going to be fine. You can go home." I was shocked. Charles hadn't been out of bed since Wednesday morning; this was Sunday, and we were just to … go home? Charles, of course, was all for it. My reluctance met his frustration. I thought that he needed at least a day to be monitored while he actually got out of bed and walked some and see how he did. Even a small heart attack can cause complications, and his was in the setting of a three-day interventional vascular procedure on his leg. It seemed it was falling to me to do all the monitoring and assessment, and while I was certainly capable of that it didn't seem that was my job. And I was already feeling the conflict between the roles of wife and physician.

I knew that he wasn't fine, but I also knew that being home was where he wanted to be and I knew from experience that home was where he was most likely to heal and recover. And so I yielded, opting to do that which would make him feel most comfortable, as we went home.

Later that afternoon, after we got Charles home and upstairs in bed, I called his own physician, Rich Rosenthal, to update him.

"They released Charles from Fairfax," I said to Rich, "the cath didn't show anything new, but he did have another small MI, based on the enzymes. They told me to take him home and exercise him."

Rich was shocked. "What? They discharged him already? How is he?" he asked. "That doesn't make sense to me."

"He is tired and in bed sleeping," I answered.

"OK, let me see him in a day or two and call me if you need anything," he responded. I thanked him and hung up, relieved that at least someone understood my concerns and was on our side.

After I hung up, I found myself moving back and forth between two distinct realities again. Charles had been in a precarious condition with this episode, and I was contemplating the medical interventions that could be brought into play. Meanwhile, as a wife, I wanted desperately for him to get through the long recovery process that lay ahead and for us to reclaim our life as we'd known it. For now, I was happy just to see him back in our bed, and our house where I knew he was comfortable. When he woke up, I knew he would want to be back downstairs by the fire, with the dog on his lap, puffing on his pipe.

But for the physician in me, the questions were piling up again. What would Charles want? How much medical intervention would he be willing to undergo if things continued to worsen? When would we need to address these issues and start to make decisions? What would his sons say? What issues were important to them?

And how would I deal with what lay ahead? This was feeling very different from our other crises. Would I know how to walk this path? What would be the issues for me? And, if it came to it, what would I ever do without him?

I didn't know. And I didn't want to think about it.

Chapter Four

· ● ● ● ● ● ● ·

So began our journey on shifting ground.

The next day, Monday, was a quiet day. I went to work and came home at lunchtime to check on Charles. He was tired and resting, but otherwise okay. Monday night, however, was not good; he couldn't sleep because he was short of breath and we were up a great deal of the night.

I went to work Tuesday with some reluctance. I wasn't sure that he would be all right, but Charles wanted to stay at home and see how the day would go. When possible, I preferred to allow him the space to maintain as much independence as possible. He didn't like being "watched," which I understood and respected. But by the time I came home at lunchtime I knew that he was in trouble. I took him to see his physician, Rich Rosenthal, who admitted him straight to the hospital. He was in mild congestive heart failure from the heart attack; he needed oxygen and needed to get some fluid off his lungs.

So there we were, 48 hours after leaving Fairfax, back at Loudoun—a week, a major hemorrhage, and a heart attack from the last time life had seemed normal.

Charles was tired, and clearly having some trouble breathing; it was hard for him to talk—even to answer the nurses' questions—as he was being admitted. Eventually, the process was completed and we were left to let him just rest.

That evening, our surgeon friend, Russ McDow stopped by to visit. Russ and Charles had become close over the years as Russ had performed many surgeries on Charles. They also shared their Southern heritage, a special almost unspoken bond between them, both Southern Gentlemen. Charles always felt comfortable in Russ' presence and trusted him completely. This was a visit I will never forget. Russ' expression was different and said everything. There was none of the typical urgency of a surgeon, rather a gentleness and calm prevailed. Sitting down in the chair beside Charles who was struggling a bit to breathe, he said, "I'm just going to sit here with you. You don't need to talk if you don't want to. I just want to be with you." That was all.

Tears came to my eyes. All that Russ, our highly competent surgeon friend, wanted to do was to be present to and with Charles' suffering, not flinching from it. It was a beautiful thing to see. And it meant the world to Charles.

Later, after he left, I ran into him in the hall. "I hated to see that, Martha," he said. "It's terrible watching Charles struggle to breathe. It makes me sad." Russ' presence was a true gift, one of the many over the years, and one for which I was, and am, grateful.

Over the next two days, Charles slowly improved. He was able to breathe better, came off the oxygen, and was starting to feel like going home. Despite the uncertain terrain we had so clearly entered, I too, desperately wanted him home. I knew that he was tired, and would be, but I wanted to have him back home, still hopeful that we had a chance of getting our lives back.

What did that mean though, to have our lives back? When I thought about it from any angle, it was clear that he probably would not return to the level of health he had enjoyed before this event. Each of Charles' medical episodes over the years, it seemed, took a piece of him that he never got back.

Still, I reasoned, if we were just able to be back home, in our space and with our routine, I knew that we could make it work. There were things that I could do to make it easier for him, and I knew that Conor would lend a hand as well. Even though Charles' other two sons lived too far away to be of daily help, their constant support by phone would be wonderfully helpful, too. If Charles didn't have to do as much, the new physical limitations would seem less significant; he could rest more and slowly get back close to where he had been. I just wanted to walk into our kitchen again and see him standing at the stove cooking or sitting at the computer writing, all the while puffing on his pipe. I didn't expect him to return to his woodworking and furniture building business yet, but longed to have him back in our house, living his life.

We were still in the hospital the next afternoon, when my friend Janelle, an ICU nurse in the hospital, ran into me and asked me if we could talk. I had known her for years. We were friends and had often worked together caring for patients. I trusted her as an excellent clinician and nurse, and her years of experience gave her a perspective which I appreciated. As we sat with our coffee, she asked, "Have you and Charles made decisions about his code status? Is it documented?"

I was taken aback. Deciding code status--meaning how far you choose to have the medical team go to try to save your life when you are dying—is something you do when someone is seriously deteriorating and/or nearing the end of life.' Surely, he isn't that seriously ill, I thought.

"No, we haven't." I answered. "Should we"?

"Yes, I think so," she said slowly, with kindness in her voice. "I know you probably don't want to hear this, but that was a bad episode and it could have turned out differently. You and I both know how quickly things can come unraveled, and if we don't know what he wants, you know we have to do everything."

Had it really been that bad, I wondered? I didn't want to think that it had, and yet, I knew full well that it had been. No one had ever mentioned this to us before, despite all the really bad medical situations in which we had found ourselves over the years. As we sat with our cups of coffee in the hospital cafeteria, I had some trouble believing that we were talking about MY Charles. I felt my body shift a bit as I wrestled with the concept. But I knew that she was right, my physician half understood completely that we needed to move forward with a discussion.

"If it would help," Janelle said, "I can come have the conversation with you both. He can begin to think about what he would want if another situation were to arise. I don't want to see you taken by surprise by something we have seen coming."

I had to talk it over with Charles, and when I mentioned it to him, he was more than agreeable to have her come. So she did. She came as an ICU nurse, as a friend, as someone who wanted us to be as prepared as we could be for what might lie ahead. What surprised me a bit was that it wasn't upsetting to talk with her, and in fact, I found it a bit of a relief. Charles did too—having the conversation gave voice to things we had each been contemplating and perhaps been unwilling to speak.

Janelle was able to talk with us in a relaxed and professional manner.

"Charles," she said, "you were in a precarious situation last week, and thankfully things turned out well. But I think we should talk about what might have happened and what you might want to consider if something like that happened again. What would you want us in the ICU to do if you are there and your heat stops? Or if you can't breathe?"

"I know," he answered. "And I understand that we should talk about my code status. I don't feel that I need to make a decision right now but I am happy to talk about it," he said. Janelle validated what had happened to Charles and was not afraid to speak about the "what-ifs." So many of the people with whom we had dealt seemed reluctant to acknowledge the gravity of Charles' situation—perhaps out of concern for us, perhaps out of fear, who knows. But it was refreshing to have someone acknowledge what was going on and what the potential issues were. Sadly, this has not been the norm in medicine. A "pre-emptive" look at possibilities and a discussion about values and wishes too often gets pushed aside for more intervention, more procedures, more heroics. And then it can be too late to make proactive choices. I was grateful for her forthrightness and honesty. We talked about the decisions to be made if his heart stopped or if he had further serious complications. It seemed clear that Charles didn't want to make any big decisions just yet, but he did seem anxious to have the conversation about possibilities. And that was a start to what ideally is a process. For us, and for many, it is a process that evolves over time. And it seems the evolving nature of the situations and the conversations helps soften the pain of having to make these difficult decisions.

We sat together and talked about the contents of a document that she had brought us, called *The Five Wishes*, and we talked about how we really needed to update our wills and get some of our personal documents, like a medical power of attorney, in order once we got home. Charles and I had talked about death before, more than once. But this conversation was different ... we had changed from abstract philosophical discussions to a specific and intensely personal conversation that seemed infused with potential reality.

The Five Wishes document is a tool that helps people identify what is important to them at the time that they are or will soon be facing their death. It outlines a series of possible scenarios and lists specific questions to be answered, which serve as a guide to help people determine some of their desires and priorities surrounding end of life care. And whereas we didn't feel that Charles was dying, it was clear that he had been in a tough spot earlier that week and that it might be prudent to begin making some decisions. As we went through the document, some of the questions seemed easy to answer, some less so.

"No, I would not want to be kept alive with a feeding tube," Charles said emphatically. "And I think dialysis, for me, would be a waste of money if my kidneys shut down. Yes, I would like to be at home to die, but I don't want to be a burden to anyone."

The document asked about comfort measures during the dying process, such as having music played or being massaged with oils. "I don't care about either of those," he answered. "They don't seem important."

It felt strange to me to be reading through a list of potential options for the love of my life's dying process, but with the oddness came a sense of relief that there was not this elephant in the room, and that we were actually talking about this. In some sense, it felt good to be able to talk about death and still have it be mostly theoretical; it felt a little less emotionally charged to me that way.

We thanked Janelle for her willingness to help us begin this conversation, knowing that there would be many more to follow. And we decided that we would address these issues again and more fully once we got home.

By Thursday of that week, I was able to bring Charles back home again, after a total of eight days in the hospital. He was expectedly tired, and spent much of the next couple of weeks resting and trying to regain his strength. Slowly, he began to get his rhythm back and our lives returned to a more normal pace and schedule.

My intuition told me, however, that this experience had been different from other illnesses and difficult medical situations over the years. There had been a palpable difference this time; this had been more severe, more intense. He had had some significant complications that could, it seemed, lead us in a new direction. Never before had someone talked with us about code status; never before had I been as worried about where this might be headed.

I found myself, once again, in a place of feeling the tension between being a wife and being a physician, a place where I had struggled in earlier years and during prior episodes of his illness. As a doctor, I understood the seriousness of these eight days. As a wife, I wanted nothing more than not to have to think about what had just occurred. I wanted it all to disappear behind us, not loom ahead of us, forcing us to think about what the future might bring.

And I was scared. This was a place we had not been before, a place that was different terrain for us to navigate. I could pretend that it was no different from his other episodes; but intellectually, and emotionally, I knew that it was. Somewhere deep inside, I knew that death was a more real possibility than it had ever been, and I was already thinking about the questions that had haunted me for years. What, in the end, happens at death? Where do we go? Is there an existence after death?

I didn't feel that his death was imminent, rather I knew that after this hospitalization, it seemed a more likely, or less *unlikely* reality than ever before. He had come pretty close. I was, and we were, going to have to learn to navigate this new landscape; at least I knew that we would do it together.

Chapter Five

·•••••••·

As March ended and we moved into Spring, Charles continued to improve, and medically, things seemed to be progressing well. At his follow up medical appointments, his physicians were pleased with his progress. He was very happy to be home, returning to some sense of normalcy in his life. The spring was becoming summer, the days were longer and the evenings gentle. We settled back into our routine, which was having our morning coffee together and then, some mornings, we would go together to my office, where Charles helped me run the practice. Since Charles had been working with me as the self-proclaimed "A.M. concierge", he would come in early with me, answer the phones and man the front desk for a couple of hours, then go home to rest. Charles and I were married while I was in medical school. He had always been a significant part of my medical life, as we had gone through my training together. He was a key part of my practice—a voice, a face and a personality known by many of my longtime patients. We loved working together, and I loved sharing that part of my life with him.

In the evenings, when I would get home, we would have our drink and talk time—sitting outside in the soft June air, watching the birds and all the emerging new growth around us. We treasured those times of being together and talking. It was the highlight of our day, and we talked about everything—the mundane things of the day, the news, the garden, the kids, what we wanted to do, what interested us, what we felt, and what we believed. Though I had always known this to be true, it was now even clearer to me—Charles was my compass, and the yardstick by which I measured everything. We shared everything; we were truly, each other's soul mates.

As is true with most illnesses, recovering from a heart attack takes time, patience and a willingness to get past your sense of fear and vulnerability. We had already had this experience many years earlier, when Charles had his first heart attack. So we were in familiar territory, but it remained a challenge to remember how much rest the body actually needs after such a physical insult. It helped to be able to give voice to those thoughts, fears and concerns, and I know that the healing process was helped by being able to talk about these things together. We were both, and each, keenly aware of the number of serious medical situations in which he had been over the years, and we knew that each event takes its toll—a slight change occurs, and things are often never quite fully as they were.

In time, we would come to understand this more fully. For now, it was enough to have him back in the house, in the kitchen, cooking, sitting at the table reading, outside watering the garden, or taking Orla for short walks. I can still see him, with his full head of white hair, long enough to curl over his shirt collar. His beard was white too; in all the years that I knew him, I never saw him without the beard. And then there were the suspenders. Red suspenders that he wore every day; with his jeans or with a tux and everything in-between. A trademark look, really. And his fleece jacket. Always the fleece, he was never not cold. I imagine that was the result of his poor circulation, but for years, even in the summer time, he tended to be cold.

By late June, he, and we, seemed really quite stable. Conor and a friend joined us for dinner one evening in late June, and I noticed that Charles was limping a bit during the evening. He didn't say anything, but by the time we went to bed, he said that he was having some discomfort in his left leg—the opposite leg from the one that had the occlusion in March.

It was a long and restless night. Charles was up and down multiple times, trying to get comfortable. Keeping the leg down, and dangling, seemed to help; it appeared that gravity increased the flow of blood to the foot. By morning, we knew that we needed to go to the hospital, and we set off for the Emergency Room yet again.

The process was much the same; he had a series of tests that confirmed the lack of good blood flow to his leg, and we were headed back to the Interventional Radiology Suite for another arteriogram and clot-busting procedure. Just as before, his cardiovascular disease was manifesting as blockages in the arteries in his legs. The lack of blood flow caused intense pain that required significant pain medication to get him even partially comfortable. Again, Conor joined me as we waited it out in the radiology waiting room—a small, inside room with no windows, that had a coffee machine and a TV that was never turned off. It was a depressing and lonely place to wait. Eventually, the radiologist came out and informed us that Charles had a significant blockage; they would again leave the catheters in place and infuse the clot busting medicine overnight.

He would be admitted again to Intensive Care and they would bring him back to the radiology unit again the next day for another evaluation.

And once again, we were on our way back to the ICU. Back to a team of thankfully familiar nurses and physicians, including Mendi, the intensivist who had been present during the near-code event several months earlier. Having that familiarity certainly helped ease the tension for us. I was worried for Charles, for his leg but also for him. To be back in the ICU, three months after the episode in March, would, I assumed, be challenging for him. I imagined that it might be hard to stay positive and to keep from being discouraged. I hated to see him back in a hospital bed with all the equipment and procedures again. But Charles handled it beautifully; he had a good attitude and was always pleasant and cooperative. He engaged with the nurses and seemed to be quite at ease with all of it. He didn't complain or resist what he was being asked to do. Other than missing his pipe and having pain that needed to be managed, he generally seemed to be all right. He rested when he could; the pain medicines made him sleepy. Conor and I sat with him for hours. We talked, dozed, listened to music; we just wanted to be together.

Things went well that first day; more clot was found during the subsequent radiology procedure, so the drugs were continued. They would take another look the following day.

At first, Charles was pretty comfortable, as the initial procedure had restored a pulse to the foot and the pain was less. But by the morning of the third day, he was becoming increasingly uncomfortable; he was restless and clearly in more pain than he had been. There was a fair amount of delay getting back to the radiology suite, but eventually we returned for the next evaluation of the blood flow in the leg.

We went through the usual routine—the checking in process, the getting ready for the procedure processes—and then finally the radiologist, Dr. Joseph, came to see him.

Charles told him that he was having pain. He pulled back the sheet to look at the leg, turned and looked at me and asked, "Where is Dr. McDow?"

He looked quite concerned; Charles' calf was very swollen and painful.

I remember thinking, how was I supposed to know where Dr. McDow was? And why? But I quickly shifted from wife to physician as it became apparent to me that what Dr. Joseph and I were looking at was a compartment syndrome—a true orthopedic surgical emergency. In a compartment syndrome, there is tissue damage that causes swelling that compresses the flow of blood and thus, seriously compromises the survival of the tissue past that point. Unrelieved, the tissue will die, and the limb is threatened.

In Charles' case, the very blood vessel that had the clot, and that they were working so hard to open up, had in fact been torn a bit, and the blood was leaking out into the leg muscle, causing the swelling and thus, the pain. A true irony, in that the very blood thinners that were being used to open the vessel and save his leg were now the cause of the bleeding that was damaging and threatening the viability of his leg.

Very quickly, both Dr. McDow and Dr. Kavanagh, the orthopedic surgeon, arrived in the IR suite to confer with Dr. Joseph. Together, they determined that an emergency surgery was essential. Over the next several minutes, I watched as this team of incredible, talented and highly trained experts assemble to take him through the next chapter of what needed to occur. Understanding the gravity of what was occurring, Conor and I were both anxious as we waited, yet again, in that radiology waiting room.

Both Dr. McDow and then Dr. Kavanagh talked to us about what they needed to do. Dr. McDow explained the challenge to the tissue, and explained the procedure. When they made the incision, the tissue would "pop" out from being under so much pressure, and that would prevent them from being able to close the wound. Closure would have to be delayed for a day or two, at least. He likened it to opening one of those cans of ready-to-bake biscuits, and how they pop when you twist open the can....

Listening to our friends, Russ and Mike, describe the procedure, I knew this was not an enviable task. For one thing, what needed to be done was risky and dangerous.

Charles had heart disease and had suffered a heart attack less than three months ago, and surgery is never a routine procedure in such a situation. For another, they would be working on someone they both knew well, a man who was the husband of their colleague to boot. Charles and I had known Mike Kavanagh since I was in medical school, where we were only two years apart. In fact, many years before, Mike was doing his internship when Charles had his open-heart surgery at Georgetown University Hospital, and he was the intern on that case.

So it was with a great deal of emotion that I watched my two friends head down the hall together, to try to save my husband's leg—*and his life.* A surge of gratitude, love, fear, pride and a host of other emotions nearly overwhelmed me then. Mostly, I felt total and complete trust, knowing that if anyone had to do this procedure on Charles, these were the two I would choose. They would do whatever they could possibly do, and that was all I needed to know.

It only took about fifteen or twenty minutes for the surgery, and soon, Charles was being taken back to the ICU. Russ and Mike had each made an eight-inch incision the length of his left calf. The wounds were open beneath the bandages through which blood was oozing. Once again, the irony struck me: he had undergone a procedure to open the blood clot in the leg and part of that process included using enormous doses of blood thinners and clot busting medicines. The vessel tore, and he bled into his muscle, causing the compartment syndrome that nearly cost him his leg. And now, he had undergone surgery to find and stop the bleeding that caused the compartment syndrome. But the wounds were not able to be closed because of the tissue swelling, and the blood thinners couldn't be stopped because of the original problem.

A complication begetting a complication begetting a further complication… I was starting to wonder where this would all end, and how many of these Charles could survive. I knew without a doubt that this was the right thing to do; it had to be done. But there was a little voice deep inside of me that was wondering and asking. In the months ahead, that voice would grow stronger, and louder, and would be met with the voice inside of Charles wondering and asking the same things.

For the next 48-72 hours, Charles bled from the open wounds on each side of his leg. He lost a lot of blood. Again and again, the ICU nurses and

I changed sheets and dressings; over and over again, Charles received blood transfusions to keep up with the losses. He was awake, but drifted in and out with pain medicines. Once again, Conor kept his brothers, Sean and Colin, up to date. He was the one who communicated with our friends and family. I was finding it increasingly difficult for me to do that, perhaps because I was exhausted, perhaps because I didn't have the bandwidth to be reassuring to them when I wasn't so sure myself what was happening. But Conor took the task in stride and was able to keep people updated.

I stayed in the room with Charles, sleeping in the chair when I could, though with his continued bleeding, there was not a lot of chance to sleep. I was exhausted, but woke early the following morning, aware of noises. Several nurses were tending to Charles, and there was an EKG machine beside him, which seemed ominous.

He was having chest pain—again—his BP was not stable and they were giving him different medications to ease the pain. He had lost enough blood that his blood pressure was low, probably the cause of the angina (pain from lack of blood flow to the heart muscle) that he was having. I guess that I had been sufficiently tired that I had slept through the first few minutes of all that activity, despite having my chair right next to his ICU bed. When I did wake up, I was instantly fully awake and alert—a skill I had learned well in medical training. Being on call, one gets used to falling asleep quickly and waking quickly too. You have to be able to respond at a moment's notice and make decisions, no matter how deeply asleep you may have been. I went from a sleeping wife to a worried physician within seconds—a dance that was becoming increasingly my norm.

Eventually, with the array of medicines and treatments available, his pain was brought under control and his blood pressure stabilized. It was a relief to know there were interventions that could, in fact, treat his condition. I didn't question what was being done then; it all seemed the obvious and right thing to do. There was a problem and it could be fixed.

Charles' situation remained tenuous for the next several days. He continued to bleed quite a lot. Eventually, Dr. McDow came to the ICU and put another stitch or two in to try to stop the bleeding. To our relief, the oozing slowed a bit after this, though Charles' vital signs remained unstable.

One morning, when his physician, Dr. Rosenthal, came to see him on his daily rounds, he was clearly concerned, and motioned me to step outside the room. An exceedingly bright internist and critical care specialist, Rich was serious and intense. He had dark curly hair, and a slightly stooped figure. Rich was direct and honest with both Charles and me and we both admired and respected him and trusted him because of that.

He wanted me to know and understand that the situation might warrant an amputation of the lower leg.

"They are doing what they need to do," he said, looking me in the eye, "but I am not willing to save the leg, only to lose the man."

My heart sank, not because of the possible loss of the leg, but because I had to acknowledge that Charles' life was precarious, which hit me like a bolt. Part of me, the physician, already knew this, but Dr. Rosenthal was talking to me as the wife. I knew I'd *needed* to hear this. I needed to know the whole— the true picture—difficult as that was.

In fact, Charles' heart was no longer stable. He had suffered yet another small heart attack during the time he was having chest pain and his blood pressure had been low—the second one in three months. And yet, Charles seemed pretty upbeat; he was still handling the situation well. He understood what was happening, it seemed to me as if he chose to ride with it and take it all in stride.

I had trouble seeing past the immediate; it was hard for me to think where this could end. In part, because I knew where it could end, in part because I was hoping that he would get better and I wouldn't have to think about what might happen. It was a continuous back and forth inside my head. I longed for stability, which seemed quite elusive.

It was on one of those evenings in the ICU when I received a phone call from my dear friend and former medical practice partner, Bob Bencze. He and his wife had just returned to the US from New Zealand; he was calling to say hi and see if we could get together in the next few days.

When I told Bob what was going on, he was at Charles' bedside with us in an hour, no longer the physician of record but ever the close friend and concerned colleague. His presence was a gift, a much-needed stabilizing force for me. Yet, a sense of stability was no longer within easy reach. It was all changing. In my heart of hearts, I knew this might not get better. And yet, my mind reached for better outcomes.

Is there anything that could be done? Anything that could—if not reverse the damage—keep him alive, out of pain and in at least reasonable condition, I wondered? I knew that Charles wasn't ready to die; he had told me that on many occasions. He was holding on to stay with us longer; he had made that clear years ago when he chose to undergo chemotherapy for his colon cancer. It was his family that was important to him, and I (and we) desperately wanted him to be able to be back home and resume his life, in whatever diminished capacity that might be.

Chapter Six

. . . ● ● ● . . .

B ob stayed with us for about an hour that evening, but was back repeatedly the next several days, both to see Charles and to be there for me. Bob's presence supported me in both roles—as wife and as physician. We had practiced medicine together for years and we knew each other "medically", which meant we could share information without a lot of words being said. Though no longer in practice, he was still a colleague in that world. His concern was palpable; it both worried me and reassured me. I knew he was someone to whom I could talk and he would understand my fears; he could also help me see the big picture when I found that difficult.

It reminded me of the time, years before, when Charles had been in the ICU following his colon cancer surgery. He had a difficult post-operative course with significant cardiovascular complications. During that time, on one particular evening, his blood pressure had been quite difficult to control. That wasn't unusual for him; his blood pressure was quite often high and hard to control, but that fact seemed lost to me at the moment. It had been a long several days; I was exhausted. I remember sitting at the nurses' station, talking on the phone with my senior medical partner Stephen, who had called to check on him. Almost in tears with frustration, I said to Stephen, "I don't know why they can't control his blood pressure."

I was worried about what might happen if they couldn't lower it. I heard Stephen's calm and strong voice at the other end of the phone say to me, "Yes you do know, Martha. He has awful cardiovascular disease." At that moment, I felt as if I had been slapped across the face back to reality. I instantly thought about the situation as a physician, and yes, in fact, I did understand what the issues were, and what would need to be done. My fears as his wife were put aside, for the moment.

Was that a good or a bad thing? Both really, and in the present situation, I was learning to hold both realities as simultaneously true. In this current instance, in the ICU with his leg issue, despite all that was happening, Charles was pretty relaxed. But he was exhausted, and that concerned me. One doesn't get much sleep in a hospital, let alone an ICU, and the lack of sleep can be cumulative and eventually, quite challenging. Being exhausted doesn't help the recovery process; I was concerned about what his recovery would be like when we would get back home, knowing that he had only just recently "gotten better" after the episode in March.

And then again, the reality of what was happening would wash over me like a wave—when I thought about what it might mean for the future, I was afraid. Afraid for him, afraid for me, afraid for us. Afraid for the future, and afraid for all that was about to change for us. And then I would remember, and try to stay present and stay away from the "what-ifs". I would remember to try just to stay present and be with him there—where we were—at that moment, and experience that particular moment. This is the essence of mindfulness, being present in the moment, staying with the experience without judgement.

Staying present—that was a challenge for me, one with which I had struggled over the years, and particularly when Charles was sick. I had the tendency to use my well-honed ability to compartmentalize and not have to deal with the intensity of the emotions at the moment, whatever the situation or emotion was.

Historically, for me, when Charles had been in serious medical situations, this had manifested in choosing, usually quite unconsciously, to be more physician than wife. It had been, quite frankly, easier to handle the situation that way. I could sit in the room, by his bedside and look at all the monitors in the ICU through the eyes of a physician, and not have to experience the emotions as intensely as when I sat there solely in "wife mode".

I had struggled with this over the years, experiencing his illnesses as *either* "physician" or "wife"— and in particular, when Charles had been in the ICU for the week after his first surgery for his colon cancer. That was a particularly difficult situation. He had been on the ventilator for several days after his surgery. When they finally weaned him off the ventilator and he awoke and was talking again, he began to hallucinate and developed a real case of ICU psychosis. He wasn't himself, his eyes had a blank stare, his words didn't make sense. I was frightened watching him like that. He was my Charles, and I couldn't not be hurt and scared by what I saw and what he said. I was his wife, and I couldn't just dismiss it all as "something that happens and will resolve," although I knew that, in my brain, to be true.

So, although it had been tempting, because it would be easier and less painful, to go through some of these experiences in physician mode, I didn't want to deny my pain and fear and I chose to have the experiences as both a physician and his wife.

Being able to switch into the dispassionately objective mode was a skill acquired in medical training. As physicians, we knew that it was necessary. But I don't recall this premise ever being discussed; we just watched it happen. In medical school, and during residency, we learned by doing. The saying was, "see one, do one, teach one." This was true not just for procedures, but we learned how to act, how to handle things by watching those above us. As an intern, there was a resident and then a chief resident ahead of me, and then the attending physician. We watched the good ones, and followed them. We quickly learned who the best ones were, the ones we wanted to emulate.

I don't recall ever having discussions about what we were feeling or experiencing; what emotions we had, we tended to keep to ourselves. There wasn't time to process what we felt about what we were doing; we just did it and kept going. We were being taught, by way of example, to be efficient at compartmentalizing; it was a terrific skill to be able to use in medical training. Being a physician, and particularly for those who perform

procedures as a part of their practice, often means doing things that cause pain or discomfort to a person—injections, incision and drainage procedures, surgery, placement of various tubes, the list goes on and on. You couldn't continue to do those things if you allowed yourself to feel the patient's pain; it was much better to compartmentalize that emotion and proceed. And besides, that is how it appeared that the residents, the chief residents and the attending physicians did it—no one ever saw them being emotional. So that was a skill to learn; don't think about it, just do it and move on.

I remember the first patient I had to declare dead. In Virginia at least, the custom was such that a physician had to pronounce a patient dead. I was a new intern, meaning that I had graduated from medical school and had been a doctor for just a couple of weeks. I was on call in the hospital and called to the room of a patient who had just died, and was asked by the nurse to pronounce her dead. I hadn't ever done that before, but assumed that I would figure it out once I got there. I got to the room and was shocked by a throng of wailing family members, some on their knees— all crying loudly. I entered the room, went to the head of the hospital bed and looked at the newly deceased person. I listened to the chest—with no heartbeat, nor respirations—it was enough to call her dead. I looked at the family members, said "I am sorry", and then I left the room. It felt bad that I couldn't do anything more for them and strange about the whole encounter.

I had witnessed death and wondered what else had occurred, other than the lack of a pulse and respirations that was the definition between life and death? What else had she lost? These were the thoughts in my head as I wrote the chart note, officially declaring her dead. This is what I wanted to discuss ... and then my pager went off and I was off to the next crisis that needed my attention. There was nothing more to be done for the dead person; there was a living person who needed help and attention. I had to shift my focus entirely and quickly. I was starting to learn to compartmentalize, like those ahead of me appeared to do; and I didn't have to think any more about the dead woman, nor the process of dying.

While this skill was a gift in medical training; it was my challenge in life. I was beginning to believe that it was not helpful to me or Charles, for me to default to this when things got tough. Once we got back home, I knew I would need to be mindful of this challenge. I would need to try to be both a physician and a wife, and allow my two halves equal space.

Struggling with this compartmentalization after one of Charles' prior hospitalizations, I had realized that I needed some help and I sought out Dr. David Begun, a wonderful and gifted psychiatrist with whom I worked over the years. It was he who convinced me to try to hold the two realities at the same time. To think that I should be able to leave the physician part of myself at the door was not a realistic expectation, he explained. I was, and am, a physician, and that is forever within me. It was not reasonable to expect myself to abandon that perspective, knowledge and experience. Nor was it reasonable to expect myself to abandon my perspective, knowledge and experience as Charles' wife. Somehow, the challenge before me was to hold each of the dual halves of my whole, to give voice to each of them and to hold them each as true.

Learning to hold two separate realities simultaneously became part of my life—physician and wife—scared about the future and yet sitting quietly beside Charles in a hospital room and enjoying just being together, grateful for any small improvement and desperately worried. Even in the hospital, we would often comment about how we were enjoying having the time together. I had mostly stopped going to my office, so we had many hours talking, dozing and just being together. Always at night we were together, alone in the hospital room between checks from the nursing staff. We treasured that time.

Chapter Seven

. . . .

Back in the ICU with Charles, now in the early summer, just three months since this series of problems had started, and with this new set of complications, in my heart of hearts, I knew a difficult truth: we were now surely on borrowed time. From a medical standpoint there was improvement, but the big picture hadn't changed much. He just wasn't likely, I had to admit to myself, to be able to continue to experience these complications and keep recovering. I was deeply worried, but then intermittently encouraged—always, it seemed, holding both truths as simultaneously true.

After several more days in the ICU, the situation began to grow a bit more stable and the decision was made to place a "wound vac" over both incisions. The wounds were still open, and would need to heal from the inside out, and the wound vac was deemed the best way to do this. Basically, it's a gauze cut to fit the wound, then a vacuum device is applied and attached to a small, portable machine that gives continuous suction. Clear plastic tubes ran from each wound on each side of his leg to the device, a small box designed to be hung from a belt or waistband. They estimated the machine would be with Charles for the next three or so months, as it slowly but surely did the job of closing the wound.

Day and night, he would be attached to it; dressings would be changed by the visiting nurses and he would need to learn how to shower around it. Having the wound vac negated the need for another surgery to close the wounds. To do that, new incisions would have had to be made and the bleeding problems might have started all over again. Most importantly, no one was anxious to subject his heart to yet another surgery and risk of further cardiac complications.

Eventually, Charles was able to get up and to move around; he was transferred to the regular floor in the hospital and there slowly began the talk of going home. He had to get a bit stronger, and the medicines had to be stabilized. He and Conor and I spent many hours together those days. Not a day went by without Conor being there, and as always, Charles would absolutely light up whenever he walked into the room.

One day, when things seemed calm, I drove back to Leesburg to check the mail, and get a change of clothes. Conor stayed with him while I headed home. The last time I had done this, Charles had almost died; so it was with some trepidation that I left. This time, I made it home and back with no disasters. But the brief interlude gave me some time to reflect. What I knew was that Charles had been sick and in challenging medical situations before—many times before. And each time he had recovered; if not completely, then enough to resume his life almost as it had been before. But this time, there had been two major events within three months, each with very significant complications. He had survived, thankfully. And all I really wanted was to get him back home and help him recover; even knowing how long a process that was likely to be. But I also knew, somewhere deep within my bones, that this degree of trouble maybe didn't bode well, and maybe this time the outcome would, in fact, be different. I had no sense that his death was imminent; rather I began to feel that it was a real possibility, and one that I could no longer quite so easily, put out of my head. I also wondered repeatedly, how much of this could he keep taking?

As we made preparations for him to be discharged back home, I had to face the changed reality of what he was physically capable of doing, and admit that I, and we, would need some help. I also knew that I was concerned about leaving him alone in the house; Charles just wasn't very steady despite working with the physical therapist in the hospital. Thinking that it would be helpful to have them there, I talked with both Sean and Colin, Charles' older sons, and asked them each to come help, which they both graciously did. They staggered their time, each spending about a week at the house with us once Charles was home. Their presence allowed me to return to my office, for Conor to be able to spend more time in his, and Charles was happy to spend time with each of them. Neither Sean nor Colin lived close by, so he didn't see them as much as he would have liked, had they been closer. Sean, the oldest, is physically large, gregarious and extroverted. He has great enthusiasm for life. Colin, Charles' middle son, is quieter, more reserved and introverted. A lover of animals, he is gentle and kind, has a cutting wit and can be sarcastic—a gift that was often used at times of tension.

Having them present with us, back in the house after Charles came home was wonderful. Conor came most evenings and we were able to spend time together; all of us: Charles, Conor, myself and Sean or Colin. We would be cooking, listening to music and talking—just being together—it felt wonderful. As Charles said to me on several occasions, "Time is becoming an increasingly precious commodity." And we were all acutely aware of the truth of that.

As was always the case, Charles was thrilled, once back home, to be back in our bed. Being able to lie together, without the noises and distractions of the hospital was a gift. Once again, we could talk about all that had happened, and he could sleep. And sleep he did—for hours at a time, getting up to come downstairs only for short periods each day. But when he did, it was wonderful to see him sitting in his chair, his pipe in hand, and to watch the lighting of his pipe … the whole ritual of that process. Cleaning the ash out of the pipe, opening the tobacco pouch and filling the bowl with fresh tobacco, then the tamping it down with the pipe tool … and the predictable cocking of his head and the sound of the lighter as he held the pipe just right so it would light. And the smell; how I loved the smell of that tobacco. I watched him sit, his long white hair curling over the top of his fleece jacket, and smiled.

But I was still very concerned about his situation, despite the great feeling of being back home and having everyone here. *How will I manage this?* I wondered though, *after Sean and Colin have gone and Conor and I are both back at work.* Charles was having a tough time eating as his appetite was poor; nothing tasted good to him as he had developed thrush from all his antibiotics. His blood pressure was increasingly erratic and he was having spells of being lightheaded and feeling weak. One evening, when he was having a lot of lightheadedness, I suggested that we might need to return to the hospital.

"You might need IV fluids, Babe" I suggested. "they might help you feel less weak and dizzy."

He declined with conviction, "No, I have no interest in going back to the hospital. Let's talk to Rich tomorrow and see what he says."

"OK," I agreed, somewhat reluctantly.

Much to my surprise, on the phone the next day, Rich, who had already made some adjustments to Charles' medications, suggested that I just keep some IV equipment at home and use it if he had another bad spell.

This was the benefit and the challenge for me, of being both physician and wife. Yes, I could do an IV at home if Charles needed it, and I knew I would, to allow him to stay home where he was comfortable. But it was hard, and felt as if it was magnifying that tension I was already feeling of being both a wife to the man I loved and a physician who had skills that could help prevent a return to the hospital. Conflict or gift? Both, really.

I know now that we were starting to make the shift, even then, to beginning to want less—not more—medical intervention. He was tired of the hospital, the procedures, the loss of himself. He was choosing for us to do as much as we could for him at home, consciously avoiding returning to the hospital. Thankfully, for us, these choices were honored and we were helped to find work-arounds. I know this isn't true for most people, and the default is to return to the hospital again and again, where the conversations about what interventions make sense for a given person, often never occur.

But it was challenging. For one thing, I was worried about how much could I do for him at home? *And even with Sean, Colin and Conor, how much could we do together,* I wondered? *And for how long? And what about after Sean and Colin had each left?*

And for another thing, the transition from the hospital to home was always a bit tricky for us. Charles held the attitude that he was "fine" and that things would be right back to normal. In reality, they weren't. He was too tired to "pick up where he left off", but he never allowed as much. He would act as if everything was fine; he never, ever, acted like a sick person. This was both admirable and frustrating; it took me longer to transition back to normal life than it did him. Whereas I would try to be protective, cognizant of all that had transpired, he would generally act as if nothing had happened. He simply adjusted his pace or his scope of activities, and carried on. It was quite amazing to witness, actually.

We had talked about it when he was undergoing chemotherapy for his colon cancer, several years earlier. I would ask him what it felt like "to have cancer inside you" and if he didn't worry that every twinge was related to the cancer. He would answer, with all sincerity, that he just didn't think about it. I came to understand and believe him that it wasn't denial; he had the ability simply to choose not to think about it. This skill served him well for a very long time. He never denied the reality of what was occurring; he would just choose to focus on other things. I know that he did think about it; we would talk for hours sometimes about all of these things. But when he chose not to, he really could choose to not think about it.

The first few days back home, with his unstable blood pressure, we were all quite anxious. Sean and Conor and I took turns being with him, as he simply could not be alone. In the evenings, we would be cooking and eating and enjoying being together, and on occasion, could even manage to forget why we were together. It could almost seem normal again. But not really. On the second or third night home, he started up the stairs, but was too weak to stay standing. He had to lie down on the landing. And there we were, literally caught on an in-between point. His fragility, and the fragility of our situation, was alarming.

For days after that, I was struck by how our "normal" was so different from what it had been; how far afield our normal had become. The events of March and June had changed our lives; our perspective and our sense of what was acceptable. Having him back home was what we wanted; so we adjusted and adapted to the new routines and the severe limitations that were the consequence of all he had experienced.

This step—"caught between what life was and what it had become"— certainly was not unique to us. Anyone whose situation suddenly changes can experience this difference, dramatic or subtle. And in the moment, I don't think that the difference is particularly noticeable, at least it wasn't to me. It was just what we did, and only upon reflection did I see how much things had changed. I knew that our prior "normal" no longer existed, but it took time to understand the full impact of that.

Slowly, very slowly, Charles got stronger and more able to do a few things. He spent a great deal of time resting, but he went back to his computer and eventually began to do some cooking. He was still attached to the wound vac, which necessitated the visiting nurse coming regularly to change the dressings. Those visits, along with medical follow up and lab work, determined much of the schedule week after week.

Eventually, he even began to come back to the office with me in the mornings, answering the phones and checking people in and out for an hour or two, at which point my office manager, George, would usually take him home and Charles would go back to sleep. I know that he loved coming to the office; having that small amount of structure and interaction with people energized him. It was wonderful for me to have him there, and I was able to share that part of my life with him, as we had always done before.

Chapter Eight

• • • • • • • • •

It was late August when the next crisis occurred; almost five months after the first one. Charles was still dealing with the wound vac and very slowly healing when suddenly one Sunday afternoon he developed a high fever. He had shaking chills and felt miserable. I called Rich who told me to take him to the Emergency Room for evaluation. Charles was a bit reluctant to go, but he agreed it was the wisest course of action. The concern was that the wound was infected and that would be very serious. After some time in the ER, he was admitted for IV antibiotics and for observation. This time he didn't go to the ICU, but to a regular hospital room, which was a nice change. He was seen by the infectious disease physician as well as his regular team. Several days into this hospitalization it was determined that the wound was not infected, and that he could go back home, again to our great relief.

This particular episode didn't have any of the drama that the two earlier hospitalizations had, but it was clear that each episode was still taking its toll. Charles was increasingly fatigued, and back home, he was less and less able to do things. When he was up and we were together, usually in the morning before work or in the evening, he would make it seem as if he were fine. He would try to cook, he would read a bit, and always, we would talk. In many ways, we were fine. We were spending time together, Conor was often at the house to visit and we weren't looking for more than that.

Eventually, the leg was healed and the wound vac came off. No longer being tethered to the devices gave him a bit of a sense of freedom. As he got stronger, he was able to increase his daily activities, but he never returned to what he had been doing in March.

It was clear to all of us that over the course of the prior six months, we had started down a different path that was taking us in a new direction. Before, Charles had always gotten better and been able to rebound. And even if not to the full measure of how he had been before, at least to a level of functioning that was acceptable and comfortable to him. This time the events just kept chipping away at him, and it seemed he would never fully recover. He simply no longer had the strength nor the stamina to do his woodworking, work outside or do much other than to read, cook some, and rest.

We had ongoing conversations about what was going to happen, and we began to talk again about the *Five Wishes* document we had started to work on back in March.

This was the document designed to help people make decisions about what they want for end of life care. After the episode in March, we had gone to our attorney to update our wills and had gotten it partially done, there were some outstanding issues that still needed to be resolved. There was an issue about a share in a property in another state that needed to be addressed that had held things up. But talking about the document again and the issue of end of life care got us thinking and talking about Palliative Care and the concept of hospice. Charles was becoming less happy with the recurrent hospitalizations and we were both questioning where we were headed. We didn't know what the right timing was for Palliative Care. Perhaps we were being premature, and I desperately hoped that we were. But I knew as a physician, that Palliative care is appropriate for anyone with a chronic illness who is likely to be in their last three or so years of life. Was he? How were we to know? The way that things had been going, part of me did believe that he was probably in his last three years of life. But some of the time he seemed just as he had always been, only more fatigued....

How was it that we had come to the point of talking about death, hospice and Palliative Care, I wondered. He was only 71, (although I think most people never think they are as old as they are) and so we wondered, was this really appropriate? While Charles was straightforward about discussing it, part of me couldn't believe that we were having this conversation and part of me knew that we needed to. I didn't know how one was "supposed" to do this, to navigate these waters. I had helped families have these conversations and make these decisions as a physician. This felt different though, because this was *us*.

I realized that there is no straight path through this thicket. We would have the most intense conversations about the future and how he wasn't really recovering and the need to start to talk about palliative care. And then we would be in the kitchen, fixing dinner or taking the dog out. Some days, he couldn't get out of bed and others he felt well enough to come with me to the office for an hour or two. I felt as if we were on an agility course, but after the prior six months neither of us was in good enough shape to be as agile or as resilient as we would have liked. And there was the stark truth; this situation was unfolding in front of us and we had no control over it or even much influence. We had to ride it as it came. All we could do was to start making decisions about how far we were comfortable and willing to go, and we didn't yet know what or where that line was or would be.

We did decide that I would call my friend and colleague Tom Sullivan, and get his perspective on the timing to begin addressing all of this. Tom was the Medical Director of a palliative care and hospice program. Tom and I had worked together teaching family medicine 25 years earlier; I trusted him and wanted his perspective.

So, the following day at work, when I had a few minutes between patients, I placed a call to Tom. It took a few days for us to actually make contact, but when we finally did have the conversation, I told him that I wanted to get his thoughts on the appropriate timing for a palliative care consult. Only then did I tell him that I was talking about Charles, but he knew. Tom said that was his assumption, because he had heard how sick Charles had been.

I described what had occurred since March, and asked, "When would be the right time to think about a consultation?"

"Now," he answered gently. "I can come over one evening and talk with you both. Tell me when."

I felt my heart skip when I heard him say "now". Though I knew in my brain that would be his answer, my heart longed for a different response. And then he went on, asking me, as he would again and again, "Martha, if you came home this evening and found Charles on the floor, do you know what you would do? And more importantly, do you know what he would want you to do?"

"I guess the truth is that I don't know. I think I know, but I am not sure," I answered.

I thought I knew what he would want, but realized that it was time to make sure.

"I think you need to make sure you know; you need to know what Charles would want you to do. I can help you talk this through, and help Charles know what some of the options are. Just let me know when we can meet," Tom said.

Several days later, in early October, Tom came by the house. The three of us sat at the dining room table. I remember it so vividly. Tom led the conversation, but he really deferred to Charles. I watched, listened and participated a little. I was a wife, a colleague, a friend and a physician—all four. Sitting in my chair at the end of the table, I watched the love of my life in his fleece jacket, puffing on his pipe, talk about his eventual death. It broke my heart.

"Charles," Tom started, "I understand from Martha what has been going on in the past six months and that you are both wondering about the future."

"That's right," Charles answered. "I don't think I am dying from all of this, but not sure I want to keep going back to the ICU. And this doesn't seem to be going in a positive direction."

"Given all that has happened recently," Tom said, "it is very likely that there will be another recurrence, and that you may well have more problems with your heart. They also might not be able to save your leg if the blockages continue to occur."

"What I know for sure," Charles responded, "is that I am not interested in heroics if the situation looks bad. I have no interest in being maintained on machines. Martha knows that."

"Yes," I answered, "you have been clear about that for a while. But if you keep having hospitalizations, the time will come when we should put some of this in writing.

"As I recall, Tom," I said, "having a living will isn't quite the same as a "DO NOT RESUSCITATE order when you're in the hospital, right?"

"That's right. If the time comes when you are sure you don't want further intervention, then you can come into Palliative care and we can leave a DNR order here in the house for you. And if you do end up back in the hospital, somehow, a DNR order can be put in place there as well. These are options that I want you to be aware of."

"I don't feel ready to make any big decisions right now," Charles said. "Nor do I feel the immediate need. I don't want heroics but I am not ready to forgo and further treatment."

"That's fine," Tom answered. "I just want you to begin to think through the options now, when you are not in a crisis. It's easier to be clear when you're not having an acute issue when decisions might have to be made quickly. And please know that I am available to you to talk this through again whenever you want."

We were clearly in the beginning stages of the conversations, and would need more time … more conversation before he was clear, or we were clear, as to what he wanted to do.

Tom had papers in the car, and was able to sign and leave for us the DNR (Do Not Resuscitate) order that people can have at home, allowing the first responders, if called, to follow that person's desire for limited treatment. Charles took it, but didn't yet sign it himself. Tom also fully described what palliative care could provide for us. Again, Charles listened and deferred making a decision. We didn't feel rushed or pushed by Tom or by the situation; we were in a relatively calm place and felt the luxury of having some time to think this through.

Tom left, agreeing that we would stay in touch and that we would think these issues through together and keep talking. That visit was a blessing. Tom had laid out the issues and the options in a way that no one else had, and facilitated the conversation.

Tom's viewpoint was different. It struck me that unlike the rest of the medical team, whose job it was to "fix" things, Tom saw Charles and the situation as being on a continuum with which he was familiar, and he could see the trajectory that we were likely to follow.

It wasn't as if Tom thought that Charles was ready to die, but his perspective was able to place him in a category of people whose outcome was likely to be a continual and further decline over the next several months, leading ultimately to death. I think that Charles and I both knew this on some level, but hoped for a different outcome. And Tom didn't pronounce the future nor the outcome, but he made space for that reality to begin to enter our consciousness and gradually to become our reality.

This was another shift; this time, though, not a shift in the situation, but rather a shift in how we were approaching it. It was a shift in our thinking, our perspective. It really wasn't a shift in our thinking, but it was "permission" to begin to give voice to what we were each thinking and fearing—an acknowledgement of what we were facing. We knew and understood that he was probably on a path that would lead to his death; the when and how were the unanswered, and unanswerable, questions.

We decided that we needed to talk this through with Conor too, and so several days later, we had the "death talk" with Conor. We had told him that we wanted to have the discussion, and why. It wasn't so much that it was new information or new territory to cover, but we wanted to include him in the discussions we were having and to get his input. Also, we had been told earlier in the week by Tom, that the data show that children do better, when the parent's death does occur, if they have been involved in these sorts of discussions and the decision making processes along the way. We had talked about death, it seemed, many times over the years, but now it was at a renewed and increased intensity, and with a new sense of urgency that we approached the topic and these discussions. And we knew we would also want to talk this through with Sean and Colin, but hoped for a chance to be able to have those conversations in person.

On the given day, Conor arrived about midday and brought lunch, as he so often and kindly did, and we talked.

"Hate to do this to you, kiddo," Charles said, smiling at Conor. "But we had a conversation with Tom the other day and we want to share our thinking with you." Conor listened attentively.

"We all know that I don't seem to be recovering from all this leg stuff; these episodes are probably going to continue. And we don't know how much more this body of mine can take. What is important to me is that you and Mom both know and understand what I do and don't want done, that I am not interested in heroics. No feeding tube … no dialysis … I have no interest in being a vegetable and having you have to come visit me like that."

"I get it," Conor replied. "I can agree with that"

"Your Dad and I are totally on the same page with this, Conor" I added. "He has been clear for a while about what is important to him and what he doesn't want."

"I would like to be at home, if possible," Charles continued.

"And if I can't communicate, I want you and Mom to be my decision makers."

"OK, Pop," Conor said. "We will." I nodded in agreement.

Watching and listening, I felt incredible pride in my son and how he was dealing with this conversation, admiration for Charles that he was able to talk with his son about his own death and I wanted to cry with the sadness of it all. I wished I could protect Conor from having to have this conversation with his Dad, but I also knew it was a beautiful and important piece of the experience. They were very close, and in many ways, this felt totally natural. I knew that this experience would ultimately become part of the fabric of who Conor was and would be. But I wanted desperately to be able to turn back the clock to the days of Legos and dogs and the little boy belly laughter that would emanate upstairs at night when he and his best friend Patrick would be watching a movie.

We got through the conversation, with laughter, some tears and mostly a being present and there, each of us for the others … and in the end, I knew that the three of us had a clearer sense of where things stood, at least for now. I knew that we would have the conversation again, probably many times, but especially with Colin and Sean when they came back again later in the fall and at Christmas time to include them in the process.

We had broken the silence and had spoken what seemed un-speakable. And in so doing, I found a freedom and a peace which surprised me a bit; along with a grief and fear that didn't surprise me.

Chapter Nine

. . ● ● ● ● . .

Over the next few weeks, Charles did fairly well, slowly getting a bit stronger.

Although still quite fatigued and taking daily naps, it was clear that he was getting better. He was engaged and interested in the things that Conor and I were doing. Always, he and I would spend the evenings and usually the early mornings together, just talking and being together. And always, in bed at night, we had more time to talk and to hold each other. Our time together was our treasure, one that we guarded at all costs. We preserved that time as best we could; it was what kept us in synch with ourselves and each other through the difficult and challenging days. When we navigated the path together, it was always less stressful for both of us. No longer able to do all the outside work that he used to do, taking care of the garden, the grass, bringing in wood, the pruning, etc., our days were centered around sitting by the fire, cooking together some, sharing our evening drink and talking ... always talking ... no matter how constricted our life became, and even when the circle of activities was, indeed, getting smaller, our time with each other was the core that sustained us through all the ups and downs of the journey.

One of the loveliest things that happened that fall was a trip that we took that Conor and Charles had planned to celebrate my birthday in mid-October. A trip didn't seem the least bit possible or even wise to me, but Conor planned and arranged it all, and before I knew it, the three of us were on a plane to Florida. We landed at the Fort Lauderdale airport and Conor had rented us a red Mustang convertible for our drive south to Key West.

The day we arrived was beautiful, bright and sunny, but quite cold and windy, which was hard for Charles. Those days, he never seemed to be able to get warm enough—always wearing multiple layers of clothing. But the scenery along the drive was spectacular, and for me, the sight of the ocean is powerful and healing in a way that not many things are.

When we arrived at the hotel, we had been upgraded to a suite; the room looked out over the harbor and was really lovely. Exhausted, Charles crawled right into bed, and Conor and I headed out to explore the town. We walked the streets, had a drink or two and ended up going out for dinner together as Charles was too tired to get up and join us.

Conor and I shared a lot that year; we seemed to do an unspoken and unrehearsed dance to take care of Charles. Conor was amazing in that he would always be in the hospital with us. Never a day went by that he wasn't there, sitting with Charles, telling him about things that were happening, talking and talking. When we were home, I don't think there was a day that went by when he didn't come by or at least call a couple of times. Conor was the one who was always able to get Charles to eat. Unlike me, he didn't ask him if he wanted something, he would fix it or bring it and distract him enough so that he ate. Their relationship was a beautiful thing to witness.

With Charles asleep in the hotel, Conor and I found ourselves at a lovely restaurant in Key West, at an outdoor table under a heat lamp. We had a few drinks, dinner, and we talked.

"I don't think we are headed in a good direction," I started. "he seems to be getting weaker. I don't think he can tolerate too many more episodes."

"I know," Conor answered. "It doesn't look good. What does Tom think?" He wanted to know.

"He doesn't think anything is imminent," I said. "But it seems clear that he thinks this is likely to continue on a downward path towards ultimate death."

"We know your Dad doesn't want any heroics, and wants to die at home, if possible. But he has also been clear that he doesn't want to be a burden to us. I think we can do it, keep him at home, when the time comes. What do you think"?

"Yeah, we can do that." Conor said, "I am sure it will be hard but we'll figure it out."

We kept talking over dinner...talking about what we were going to need to do to provide support for Charles, acknowledging how much things had changed in the past several months. It was a gift to be able to have this conversation and to be able to speak openly and frankly together about the future. I appreciated Conor's ability and willingness to talk, and to share his feelings.

On Saturday, Charles did get up and the three of us went out in the middle of the day. We had lunch at Margaretville; one of the best pictures we have of Charles and me is one that Conor took there. That evening, we went on a sunset harbor cruise, which despite the incredible wind and cold, was wonderful. Sunday, we packed up, drove back up the coast, and flew home—back in our own house and bed after just three days.

Within the week, Charles was back in the hospital; the leg again occluded and was in need of another interventional radiology procedure to open the blockage. This time they were dealing with an aneurysm above the graft as well as occlusion farther down the leg. After another five or so days in the hospital, most of it in the ICU, they were eventually able to get the blockage opened and blood flowing again. Charles was tired, and getting tired of all of this. The physicians were warning us that the remaining options for the leg were becoming fewer.

What was the right thing to do? I found myself wondering again. This being the fourth time he was having this procedure in nine months, it was hard not to wonder what would be the outcome of all these recurrences. What options would we be presented with? And how do you start to make these decisions? We had been lucky again; the occlusion had been successfully opened, but what would be next? Would there be another occurrence? Would there be more complications? How much more of this could he take? These were the thoughts going through my mind as we sat in the ICU and waited.

Meanwhile, he became disoriented in the ICU, confused as to why he was there and what was going on. One horrible long evening, he was even angry at me. I know that he was angry at the circumstance, but it made me feel sad and afraid and very alone in the situation. It is not uncommon for people to get confused in the hospital—days and nights blend without long quiet periods for sleep, there are medications, noises and procedures that are unfamiliar; in general a stressful and exhausting process. So, confusion is common, yet very hard to witness. And in this case, it was hurtful, although I know that wasn't his intent. By morning and after a little sleep, the confusion and thus the anger had lifted, and he was more himself again. I was grateful for that; it lessened the stress for me enormously.

Tom came by during that hospitalization. He had heard that Charles was back in the hospital and he just stopped by to talk. Although he knew that this event was taking us one step closer to palliative care, he still didn't push. He did, however, remind us that it was an option.

Again, in a conversation out in the hall, Tom asked me if I knew what I would do if I came home and found Charles unconscious, and more seriously, if I knew what Charles would *want* me to do. I had to admit that I really didn't know for sure. I had a good sense, but nothing was yet in writing. I knew that despite having started those discussions, it was clear that we still had a lot of work left to do. Our work with the attorney after the events of March had stalled out over an unresolved technical issue, and probably our shared denial. So we still hadn't even finished updating our wills, power of attorney, and other documents. I think the truth is that we just hadn't chosen to face facts that fully and specifically yet. And we could probably rely on our old wills, so we didn't really feel pressing urgency.

After Tom left, I found myself again trying to balance the two realities I was witnessing. On the one hand, this latest crisis seemed to have resolved, or to at least to be heading that way, and then we were talking about wills and palliative care. I knew and understood the need to hold each of these realities; improvement and palliative care discussions, as true, but it was hard. I often felt as if I was walking on a tightrope.

Whenever we talked about it, Charles seemed usually to choose the place of being positive and upbeat. He would say that he was fine; he would do as much as he could.

"I am fine," he would answer when anybody asked. "Why not?" was his signature response.

"*Really? I could give you twenty reasons,*" I would answer in my mind. But having that positive outlook served him well and allowed him, I believe, to keep going.

When fatigued, he would stop, sit down or rest, take a nap or whatever he needed to do to recharge. He knew the reality. I knew he wasn't denying what was happening.

Rather he seemed somehow to rise above it and refused to give in. He never wallowed in self-pity, he never bemoaned his situation. He would be sad about the future, but grateful for the moment. He had a way of being present that I admired.

Charles seemed to accept his situation with incredible grace—he moved into his new space of diminished physical capacity elegantly. He went on with his life the best he could, letting go of those things he could no longer do.

I was, perhaps, less graceful in watching it. I ached for him and for what he could no longer do. No longer was he able to do his woodworking, which for years had been his livelihood, making handmade furniture and cabinets. Years ago, I used to watch in awe as he carried sheets of plywood, lifted rough-cut planks to run through the planer, load heavy items onto his truck. I don't know if he ever realized how physically strong he was, especially his arms. Those same arms that would cut firewood, build our terrace and our kitchen cabinets … those incredible hands that would cook a fabulous meal, draw his architectural plans, paint landscapes and year after year, light that pipe, hold me. But when he was no longer able to do those things, he seemed to move from them without a lot of regret or looking back, as least externally. Inside, I knew that he couldn't help but hurt, though he appeared to be able to let go with grace.

Charles was finally discharged home the night before Thanksgiving, and the three of us had a quiet Thanksgiving together. Most of the focus for the next couple of weeks would be on our Christmas Party.

Chapter Ten

· · ● ● ● ● · ·

For 30 years, Charles and I had held our annual Christmas party; an open house where we usually had 100 plus people; friends from over the years from all different parts of our lives. People loved the party; it had become an institution in itself, and they looked forward to it year after year. There had been several occasions over the years when it probably would have made sense to cancel it, but we never did. Charles' "MO" was to carry on, no matter what, so carry on we did.

This year, however, we seriously discussed canceling it, because it was simply an enormous amount of work. It usually took weeks to organize and plan, and about a week for Charles to do most of the cooking and preparations. We simply didn't have that amount of time; nor did he have the energy. In the end, after a lot of discussion, we decided to proceed, but do less of it ourselves, buy more prepared food, and let other people help.

The night came, and it was magnificent. I felt the poignancy of it before it even started. Charles glowed; he was rested after a nap, and thrilled, I think, to be home in the house, holding court in front of the fire, pipe in hand; red suspenders as always. We had decorated the house as usual, with our many, many nutcrackers, the tree in the living room all decorated and lighted. The trio that had played at the party for the prior twenty years were ensconced in the library and the house was filled with the lovely sound of their music. Charles sat in his chair by the fire, yielding his usual greeting of everyone and trying to tend to everyone's needs.

It was interesting for me to see him yield as he did. This very independent man allowed others to help; food to be pre-prepared, others to do much of the preparations. He had always been so proud of the party and of the food; his smoked salmon, smoked turkey, beef tenderloin, country ham … it went on and on. But he knew he didn't have it in him to do it, and he yielded. Charles was so "on" that evening that my face was sore from smiling. It was a wonderful gift that he was so happy and felt well enough to participate; he talked with so many people and could reconnect with friends he hadn't been able to see all year.

Both of Charles' older sons, Sean and Colin came for the party, Sean bringing one of his daughters with him. It had been years since all three brothers had been home for the party; it felt like old times for us. I am sure that it had been hard for Sean and Colin not to have been able to be present with their Dad during each of the episodes in the past year, and I was sure it was hard for them to see such a change in their father. Things were clearly different. But as I watched, they each stepped into the new rhythm gracefully, and I knew that it meant a great deal to Charles to have us all together.

It was a glorious night and though we all knew on some level that it was likely to be our last Christmas Party, everyone, I think, just decided to enjoy and savor the moment. And we did. Charles spent hours talking and reconnecting with old friends, enjoying the food, the music, the electricity in the air—everyone seemed happy. It was, as he said later, a triumph.

The morning after the party, Charles wanted to have a talk with all of us together. He wanted to be able to talk through his thoughts about end of life care, as we had done with Conor the previous month. He had been thinking, and writing, about this for several weeks. So we gathered in the living room; Charles, myself, Sean and his daughter Becca, Colin and Conor, and Charles began to talk, as he put it, "about my inevitable death".

"We know that my death is inevitable," he said. "I just hope it's not soon. But I want you all to know what I do and don't want when that time comes."

Again, he reiterated, "I have no interest in being kept alive on machines, no heroics. No feeding tubes, no dialysis, no respirators. When I die, I will die; no prolonging it, please. Oh, and when I die, I want you to say I died. I am not going to "pass"; I am going to die. You can donate my body to science, but I doubt they would accept it at this point." And I would like, if possible, to be at home."

There was some nervous laughter, and Conor broke the tension saying," You know, we could have you taxidermy-ed and just keep you in your chair."

We all laughed, and the conversation got easier after that. Perhaps not easier, but less hard. Perhaps because I had already experienced it with Conor, but the raw pain of it seemed less this time; I think we were all on some level prepared for it. And we were all aided by Charles' ability to be direct and honest and clear about what was important to him. It was quality of life, not quantity that mattered to him, and there was absolute clarity, understanding and agreement about that at the end of the conversation.

Can you get used to or be good at these conversations? Maybe so.

Charles' ability to have this sort of conversation with his family was aided, I believe, by his interest in recent years, in telling the story of his life and in becoming increasingly direct in what he said. No longer interested in "pretty-ing" things up; he was inclined to speak his truth in a raw, and sometimes painful way. As he'd gotten older, he was more and more interested in being direct with what he thought and felt, and he didn't want any of us to hide from the truth. One of the things he did in the last few years was to write his memoirs. He worked for years, writing many if not most days for a couple of hours. It started out as a project to tell his three sons the "who, when and where" of his early years, but it ended up being more of the "how and why", an explanation of how he had navigated his life. It was factual and somewhat opinionated, but never apologetic. He wanted to explain the choices he had made, and the things that he had done, so that his sons would someday be able to have an understanding of their father. He told it all—the good and the bad.

Likewise, when Charles was sick, he wanted to be direct and honest about his situation. So we talked and talked about it; over and over again. We talked about what we knew, what we didn't know, what we feared and what was important to each of us. It was in this talking, the open and honest discussion of what was happening, that we were able to navigate the path ahead of us as we did.

Perhaps then, not unexpectedly, for several weeks, Charles had been writing about his wishes for the end of his life. This really became the template for the conversation we had as a family, the morning after the Christmas party. By the end of that conversation, there was both an acknowledgment and acceptance of where we were and a slightly clearer sense of where we were heading.

The rest of the day was less intense; we simply enjoyed each other's company and the chance to be together. We filled the days that followed with Christmas preparations and spending time with Colin, who had come out for the party and stayed a few days after that. They were good days, enjoyable for the time we spent talking, reflecting, and making each moment count.

In the days that followed the family "death conversation" as we began to call it, there was more talk about death, as if an unspoken prohibition had been lifted. The topic seemed less frightening, less foreign. It was during this time that Charles began to reflect on the difficulty he was having with the notion that perhaps the reason that he hadn't yet died was because his "work here was not complete", as he had been told by quite a few people in these past months. Time and again, we had heard people make that comment to him and their surprise that he was still around. It always felt jarring to me, as if someone was invading a private space where they had no business being, but I suspect that it was not ill intended. I hated to see Charles being put in what seemed like the defensive place of trying to explain that he was still alive, though, and it always bothered me to hear those comments. The question, though, was an interesting one, and opened some interesting conversations for us.

"Maybe they are right," he said to me. "Maybe I haven't died yet because I don't know what it is that I am supposed to be doing, to have done."

It was clear that this felt burdensome to him, and I found it painful to watch him struggle with this concept and ask repeatedly, "I wonder what it is that I am supposed to have been doing"?

As I sat with this question and reflected, I found myself getting more clear about it. It was becoming clear to me that it was the process of facing his death head on and dealing with it that he was teaching us, and that this was the work he was supposed to be doing.

"It seems to me," I said, "that your work is teaching us all, all of us here, about death and about the dying process. You're teaching us how to do it, Babe, with such courage and grace. I love you."

"I love you too," he answered, "and maybe, you're right."

He was teaching us all… my dear Charles, ever the teacher in my life and for all these many years. I remembered first meeting and getting to know Charles, many, many years before, when he was my teacher in school; and how, for so many years he had been teaching; on so many levels and in so many ways. As the art history teacher in my high school, Charles and I had developed a deep friendship which, years later, would form the basis for our love and our marriage. It's how I first fell in love with him, and it occurred to me that maybe it would be how he would leave me too—still teaching ….

After such a lovely Christmas party where we had all been together, and after Sean and Colin had left to go back home, my mother came to visit and to spend Christmas with us. It was a lovely Christmas, and she, Conor, Charles and I spent long quiet days together in front of the fire. My mother, then in her late 80s and not as physically strong as she used to be, was nonetheless mentally perfectly intact and she and Charles loved to sit and talk. They were gentle days; Charles was tired and sometimes seemed to drift off, but it was a warm, relaxed, family time that we all enjoyed.

During those weeks around Christmas, I began hearing Charles talk during the night. It sounded different from how it had sounded periodically over the years when he would occasionally talk in his sleep. This sounded somehow more significant; it was conversational sounding, even from just one side of the conversation.

Lying there in the dark, I knew that his words were not directed at me, so I usually would not respond. Occasionally, if I did, it seemed that the sound of my voice would disrupt the conversation and it would stop. In the morning, I would ask Charles if he knew he had been talking.

"You were talking in your sleep last night," I said one morning.

"I know, but you didn't answer," he said.

"Oh, I didn't think you were talking to me"

"I am not sure," he said." I can't really explain it, but I feel as if I was somewhere else."

"Do you know where? Who was there?" I asked, fascinated by what he was describing.

"No. I can't tell who they are, but the people feel familiar...and it's not frightening or disturbing at all. It actually feels quite pleasant," he said on one of the mornings after he had been talking again during the night.

"I think I was in another dimension" he said.

He didn't look the least bit upset by this. It felt odd but significant to me, and I felt great relief that he seemed so comfortable with the experience.

My mother left at the end of the Christmas week, and Charles and I had a few lovely quiet days together. New Year's Eve, for us, was magical—though we no longer cared much about celebrating. That night, we had a magnificent evening of being together, feeling close and intimate; we fell asleep—both of us happy in each other's arms.

Chapter Eleven

• ◦ ◉ ◉ ◉ ◦ •

Several hours later, Charles was awake with leg pain again. We were up and down all night, trying to postpone the inevitable trip back to the hospital. We both finally fell asleep in the very early hours of the morning when he had some short-lived relief, but woke a couple of hours later, knowing that something had to be done. So, for the second time in our almost thirty years of marriage, we spent New Year's Day in the ER and then the ICU. The first occasion had been many years earlier, when he was admitted for angina that was progressing and there was concern of a heart attack. This time it was his leg that again was compromised by lack of good blood flow, just as in each of the other episodes earlier in the year.

The occlusion in Charles' leg had recurred, and they started again with the protocol for breaking up the clot with blood thinners. In one sense, we were in very familiar territory, as we had done this same drill already four times in the past ten months. At the time, I didn't feel particularly afraid or worried about it. In another sense and on a deeper level I knew that this couldn't continue. The radiologist was already saying that we were at a point where there wasn't much else left to try; it was increasingly likely that he would lose the leg. Charles understood that possibility but was willing to have them try again to open the blockage.

As we sat in the ICU again that day, I struggled to stay present with the actual situation and not wander off into the land of "what if". Staying present was hard. It is a great antidote to fear and anxiety, but something that is hard to do in a crisis. For me, it was an ongoing challenge and something I needed (and still need) to practice frequently. Being present in the moment, and focusing your attention on the here and now, being mindful, is a technique used by many to deal with anxiety. If you are truly in the present, it's virtually impossible to be also in the future in fear and anxiety. I didn't know if I would be able to be successful in staying focused and present; I knew I needed to try.

As we sat and waited in the ICU, I felt conflicting things—on the one hand things were sort of at a standstill; we were again in the process of waiting to see how events would unfold, and all we could do was wait it out. On the other hand, it felt as if we were on a path tumbling out ahead of us that we couldn't stop, or really even influence. And again, for a short moment that day, I felt real fear. It flooded over me suddenly, along with a real sense of foreboding. It formed a pit in my stomach—a bodily fear that was short lived, but reminded me again of the precariousness of the situation. I knew that we had already way passed the odds with all the procedures on the leg in the past several months as well as his underlying heart disease but struggled with the fact that much of the time he didn't seem that sick. A different person, one without the intense resilience that Charles had, might not have been able to be as positive as he was, and the actual reality of the situation might have been clearer to see. That Charles could seem not to be that sick was, in part, because that is how he *chose* to be. But he was sick, and I couldn't deny the reality that was staring at me, yet I didn't want to acknowledge it either.

I began to think seriously about the possibility of losing Charles, and wondering what that would be like. Not the actual process of losing him, which I thought at least my physician half knew and understood and could imagine, but rather the reality of having him gone. That, I couldn't imagine. It occurred to me then that there are two distinctly different "afterlives"—

one for the person who leaves, one for the person left behind. I hadn't ever thought in those terms before, but it struck me then that both of those do exist, and each seemed lonely and daunting in its own way. It seemed to me that the afterlife for the one who leaves somehow seems lighter, perhaps even easier, than the one for the person left behind.

After several days, the blood flow in the leg had been restored and he was able to be transferred out of the ICU. Once again, we had been lucky, the procedure had worked. *But what*, I wondered, *was ahead of us?* We couldn't keep having this dire scenario repeat every two months. Sooner or later it seemed, we would have to make a different decision; the choices would have to change. I didn't know how much more he could take, and found myself wondering if it was finally time to introduce a totally different discussion, a discussion about choosing to do less intervention. We had broached the subject intermittently over the past several months, had had discussions with Tom, but those conversations still seemed mostly theoretical to us. Now it seemed we needed to revisit the subject with a renewed intensity and sense of reality. Clearly, we were in a new situation; the shifting ground beneath us was continuing to erode and stability no longer seemed part of our reality.

I was in my office on Wednesday afternoon, when Mendi, the intensivist physician in the ICU, called to say that they were moving Charles out of the unit to the regular floor. He was doing well, since the blood flow to the leg had been restored and that he no longer needed to be in the ICU. He would go to the regular floor for a day and then go home. That was great news, and I was excited to hear it. When I got back to the hospital at about 6pm, as he was about to be transferred, I knew instantly that he wasn't quite right; something intangible was "off". Charles' blood pressure was quite elevated, but other than that, by the numbers, he looked okay. His nurse, Debbie, however, told me that she was concerned; he hadn't seemed quite right to her either. Despite our misgivings, he was transferred to the telemetry unit, and within an hour of getting into the room, he was short of breath, his oxygen dropped and he was clearly struggling. He had a fever and he felt unwell. Mendi was paged and came back to see him. He was given oxygen and a diuretic to remove fluid; both of which seemed to help a bit. After that the night was fairly uneventful, but I was on high alert and kept one eye open most of that night, watching him.

The next morning, his left knee was swollen, sore and red. We were afraid that the joint itself had become infected or that he had an infection of the skin, a cellulitis, He was seen urgently that morning by Dr. Kavanagh, our orthopedist friend, who started Charles on very broad spectrum antibiotics for a presumed cellulitis. He didn't think that the joint itself was infected, to our tremendous relief. A skin infection is much simpler to treat than an infected joint and I was grateful not to have Charles have yet another complication.

The next few days were incredibly challenging, and I suspected that was because we were both coming from a place of very low reserves. I was tired; he was physically and mentally exhausted. His body had been through so much, including five ICU stays in nine months. Neither of us had much resilience left, and we were vulnerable, on all levels—body, mind and spirit.

The evening after starting the new antibiotic medications, Charles was obviously exhausted and still did not act quite himself. My assumption was that it was the infection, and that it would just take time. But that night, after Conor had left and we were alone in the room together, his behavior got increasingly strange; he was obviously seriously confused. He could pull it together and seem all right when the nurse came in to check on him. But he wasn't alright. His confusion worsened dramatically throughout the night. He didn't sleep and he talked all night, not making any sense. He was utterly confused about where he was, what the equipment was, everything about his circumstances. It was a seemingly endless night, trying to keep him distracted enough not to remove the IVs or the oxygen.

Something fundamental had changed and I could see it. He didn't look like himself; his eyes had a vacant look, as if he weren't there. He was reaching for things that weren't there; going through the motions of drinking tea, with no cup nor any tea present (what we would come to call drinking air-tea), lighting a pipe that was not there either.

He would say words, but they had no understandable meaning, at least not to me.

By morning, I knew that we were in trouble. I called Conor to update him and once again, he quickly arrived to be with us. Charles' physician Rich Rosenthal came by, and Charles was unable to tell him where he was, the date or almost anything. An emergency CT scan of his head and blood work revealed no specific cause of the confusion. He was deemed to be suffering from an acute delirium; he remained terribly confused. He was agitated and couldn't sleep. At this point he hadn't slept since Wednesday evening; it was Friday afternoon and he seemed to be getting worse.

During that day, several of our physician colleagues stopped by. It was hard for me to watch the looks on their faces; everyone was alarmed by his condition. An acute delirium has a statistically high mortality rate, and we all knew it and were all scared. At one point, my friend and practice partner Stephen Napolitano stopped by and said he would stay in the room with Charles while Conor and I could go get something to eat, which we did. We were gone just a few minutes, and when we came back, Stephen was there, along with Dr. Rajendra (Raj), his oncologist, who was hand feeding Charles some bites of ice cream, encouraging him each step of the way. It was a bittersweet moment; the tenderness was profound; the fear was palpable. Charles kept reaching for tea that wasn't there and trying to light his pipe, which also wasn't there.

Finally, in almost desperation, I climbed into the hospital bed with him, wrapped my arms and legs around him and held him tight. I told him that we were going to take a nap, and after I was able to convince him that he didn't have to get up to go get in the bed; that we were, in fact, already in bed, he relaxed into my arms and finally fell asleep. He slept for three or four hours, and when he woke up, the confusion had partly lifted. He was able to sleep on and off that night, but would still drift in and out of confusion.

I didn't know why this was happening, why he was delirious. No cause had been found, but his confusion remained very real. There isn't always an explanation for a delirium, and dealing with and accepting the unknown was hard. What I did know was that I was scared. This crisis was different from all the cardiovascular crises that we had endured over the years. I knew that landscape, but this was new and frightening territory. In many ways, I felt as if he had gone; this was not my Charles and it was exceedingly difficult to witness. I knew too, that he needed me there to keep him as grounded and oriented as possible, which I did. But I was worried this time, in a different way from before.

Where, I wondered, *were we headed?* The ground was shifting again; and I started to wonder, once again, about how one knows when enough is enough. I was thinking about Tom and our conversations about palliative care, and wondered how it is that one actually steps into that place of making decisions about limiting further care. I knew, as a physician, how to make the referral; I didn't know as a wife how to do it, or when. And I wondered, *were we at that point? What would he want?* I knew, from the conversations we had had, what he didn't want; on that I was clear. But perhaps this was still premature, perhaps the confusion would clear completely and we would be back to just having the leg to worry about … maybe we wouldn't have to face it quite yet.

In discussing a prognosis or palliative care with patients and their families, there is often a fear that people might give up too soon, that they might get better and wish they had continued care. Sometimes, the important discussions get put off fearing that someone "isn't ready". But understanding is key, and to me, what seemed important was to have the knowledge of the options and to have an understanding of the landscape in which these decisions are made. That is what Tom had provided for us and each of our prior conversations made the subsequent discussion feel less foreign. I had to admit to myself that the landscape had been drawn for us, it was time to take action and make some serious decisions.

That afternoon, as Charles slept for a few hours, I called and talked to my sister, Sara. Updating her as to what was going on, she sensed my fear and she drove down from Boston that night, to be with me. She got in about midnight; it was wonderful to see her and to know that she was there. I made her a bed of sorts on the pull-out chair in his room; I was "sleeping" in the reclining chair by his bedside, as was my custom, or I would get back in Charles's bed with him whenever he got confused and hold on to him, which seemed to help.

Chapter Twelve

． ● ● ● ● ● ． ．

The next day, Charles' mental state was fairly clear, except when he was fatigued, which is when his confusion would increase. After a day of visiting and of Conor, Sara, Charles and me having dinner together in the hospital room, Conor left for home, and we settled in to go to sleep.

It was about midnight when I woke suddenly; not quite knowing why.

In the space of a couple of seconds, the nurse came in and woke Charles to ask if he was OK. He said that he was, and seemed to go back to sleep. She told me that on the monitor, his heart had had a major ten second pause, and they were bringing in the "Life Pack", the resuscitation equipment, so it would be available if the pause recurred. I asked her to show me the strips from his EKG, which she did. There on the strip was, in fact, a very long, ten second pause, where he had not had any heartbeat at all.

Instantly I was in physician mode, knowing fully the implications of what had occurred and the likely scenarios that would occur if his heart stopped again. I knew that he didn't want to be "coded" (resuscitated). He had been clear about that. I knew that he didn't want to have CPR and be put on a breathing machine. But this situation was challenging because we didn't know the cause of what had just occurred. Could it have been a simple issue that would respond to a medication, or did it signify a more serious cardiac issue? Had he had another heart attack? Would it happen again? Sara and I talked about it and I called Conor and talked it over with him. Charles was sound asleep and seemingly oblivious to what had just happened.

I knew that I didn't want to have him be coded and believed that he didn't want to be either. I had to struggle with that fact that meant we were talking about taking an action, or rather an inaction, that could likely result in his death. How can you want two opposite things simultaneously? I didn't know how to do that. I had to remember the words of my psychiatrist, David Begun telling me to try to hold the two parts of the whole at the same time, my physician self and my wife self, and to allow for them each and to honor then both. Now I needed to hold these two parts of the whole, wanting him not to die and honoring his desire not to be resuscitated, allowing for them both and honoring them both. I felt heartbroken and scared, but also deeply wanted to honor his desire not to be coded. I loved him enough to be willing to say no to that which could keep him alive, if only for a while.

After talking it over with Conor, I went in and woke Charles up and had one of the hardest conversations I had ever had with him. I had to tell him that his heart had stopped for 10 seconds, and that if it happened again, they would resuscitate him and restart his heart, "code him", and I had to ask him if that is what he wanted. Although having been clear about his intentions with his family, as a patient in the hospital, he had not had a DNR in place. Up to now, he had chosen each time, to continue with the interventions for his leg.

"If your heart stops again, you know that they will have to do CPR to try to resuscitate you, right?" I asked him

"I don't want that," he answered. "You know that"

"I do … then we should ask them to call Rich and get a DNR if that's what you want. Do you want me to ask them to do that"?

"Yes, that's what I want," he replied, and he seemed to drift back off to sleep. So Rich was called, and he and I spoke and he agreed to give the order.

After having the DNR order placed on the chart, the nurses removed the life pack from the room and Sara and I sat there watching Charles sleep; probably eventually falling asleep ourselves … me wondering if we had just done the right thing, but feeling strongly that we had. That it signified the beginning of the next significant chapter I hadn't quite yet grasped.

I felt strongly about the DNR, because I knew that he was at a place where resuscitation was unlikely to make a significant impact. True, the doctors could have been kept Charles' heart going, had his heart stopped again, but to what end? Perhaps whatever had caused his heart to stop could have been remedied, but that would have neither fixed nor addressed the underlying problems of the recurrent leg obstructions. We needed to look at the situation in context, not just as a series of isolated events that were unrelated to each other.

It is true that no physician can tell a person how much time they have left, and physicians often will tell people that statistics don't mean much. Each person is unique, and there are many factors that play into how long a person might survive, and that two people with the same diagnosis might survive very different amounts of time. There are factors that influence a person's survival that we know and understand, and many more that we don't understand at all.

It was clear, however, that Charles was now in a place of progressive decline.

Tom had told us that several months earlier, and he had experienced another two hospitalizations with multiple procedures and significant complications since then. It was not likely that he would suddenly get better and, in fact, was very likely that he would continue to have recurrences of his leg occlusions. His cardiovascular system was in bad shape, and he was at extremely high risk of having ongoing cardiac events. All this now with the delirium that had not yet fully cleared. I couldn't deny it any longer; we were at the place where decisions had to, and were in fact, being made.

The rest of the night was mercifully uneventful. Charles seemed to sleep fairly well. Sara was off at the crack of dawn; a snowstorm was predicted and she wanted to get out in front of it. I couldn't stand to see her go; I felt scared and lonely… but I had to get back to the room and be present with Charles.

The morning was filled with his various physicians making rounds and discussing the events of the night before. There were lots of opinions offered, and then the suggestion was made to put in a pacemaker to prevent Charles' heart from stopping again.

I was aghast at the suggestion and had a strong, visceral reaction. I couldn't believe what they were suggesting. At the very least, putting in the pacemaker meant yet another procedure/surgery, for which he would be at significant risk. But more important was the fact of what they were offering: a way to keep his heart from stopping again. I said, in response, "I can think of one possible, kind outcome for this man as we look forward, and that would be for his heart to stop quietly. Why would we remove that possibility?"

"It is a fairly simple, straightforward procedure. One that will prevent what happened last night from recurring. Of course, you would want to do that?" the cardiologist asked.

I responded, "How likely do you think it is that he will have another cardiovascular problem?" And the answer I received was that "it was not a matter of if but rather when." Everyone seemed to agree that the odds were distinctly not in Charles' favor, but no one was willing to suggest that perhaps we should start thinking about different options. I believed that the time had come to consider, and seriously think about choosing comfort care and to stop trying to fix what was wrong.

For the rest of the day and night, I wrestled with myself over this. I was torn between wanting to believe that there was a good, medical solution and knowing deep down inside that there was not. I was frustrated and even hurt, in a strange way, feeling almost betrayed by a medical system seemingly unable or unwilling to deal with this very difficult situation. I was enormously grateful for the repeated heroic procedures and interventions that his physicians had done to save Charles' leg and life, for the superb medical and surgical management that had gotten him this far. But suddenly, I felt as if no one was looking at the "big picture"—the entire man. Each person on the team was focused on a part, and was doing their best to make that part well ... but I was afraid that we were losing sight of the man along the way. What was the significance of the pause? What really was his prognosis? Was it time to take a different approach? Was it OK to continue on in this process, and if so, what was the goal? I felt almost as if we were going to keep flailing at him until there was nothing left. And that might be the plan, agreed to by all, but I hadn't heard anyone gathering the team and having that discussion.

Had it not been for my initiating the conversations in the fall with Tom, Charles and I wouldn't even have really known about the options of palliative care. And I wondered, *was there a goal in this process? And if so, was the goal just to keep him alive at all costs? What were his goals? What did he want? Where was the concept of the "quality of life?"* When would the time come to stop and pause, and begin to talk about what was really going on? Maybe Charles would have been interested in continuing to push hard for every possible intervention that existed, and perhaps not. But no one had stopped and asked him.

I didn't know how I could be at such odds with the team of my colleagues who had worked so hard for him and for us, and I realized that my sense that we should not intervene with a pacemaker could mean "allowing" him to die. How could I be pushing for that choice? Was I? The conflict in me was tumultuous, and yet I had a very strong sense that a pacemaker was not the right decision. I just didn't see that it would solve anything and I sensed that it was time to focus on the quality of life, not just the quantity.

I tried hard not to influence Charles as we talked about it; it was a decision that he would need to make, and one with which he would need to be comfortable. Ultimately, he was the one who would have to live with, and perhaps die with, this decision.

What I wanted for him, and ultimately for us, was to have happen that which would be in his highest and best interest. And in this case, I believed that meant not to intervene with a pacemaker. Let me be clear, it wasn't the pacemaker itself that concerned me. It is not a difficult procedure, nor a particularly challenging device to have inside of you. For me, in this case, it was the process and what it symbolized. I felt as if we were on a medical moving sidewalk that would just keep going, whether or not it made sense to do so. There were always more options—the pacemaker, an amputation, further interventions—any of which would be fine and appropriate in some cases. But the question remained, what was appropriate for Charles? That's what I desperately wanted discussed, and answered ….and the conversation was never even initiated.

Later that Sunday afternoon, after the physicians' rounds were done, Conor had left to go home for a while, and Charles and I were alone in the room, we were able to talk. His confusion had cleared and he was cognizant of the events of the prior several days. I was on the bed with him, and we held each other and both cried … and talked. He finally said to me "I don't think I have much time left. I don't want to be in the hospital anymore, I want to go home" At the same time, Charles told me that he didn't want to have a pacemaker; he would do the adjustment of medication that had been suggested as an alternative and then see how he felt. His goal was clear—to get home.

Interestingly, later that afternoon, Tom stopped in to visit. He was in the hospital making rounds and saw that we were still there. The three of us talked for a while, he was very supportive of Charles' desire to get home and to put off any further intervention at this point. He again offered help from the palliative care/hospice team, which Charles accepted. We agreed that they would make a visit within a day or two after we got home, which, by the time that everyone got organized and on the same page about the plans, would be another two days off.

It was clear that some of Charles' physicians were surprised by his decision to go in the direction of palliative care, but again, when pressed, none of them could articulate a reasonable likelihood of him having a good outcome or a real improvement.

And so it was that we had come to the fork in the road and had chosen the path of less intervention. Charles had chosen to go home, in keeping with his wishes that he had so clearly articulated to us as a family in the months before. He hadn't chosen to forego any and all treatment, but he had chosen to decline a pacemaker insertion at this time. He was, I realized, slowly moving farther down the path; closer to the end. His ability to make this decision, and many more that would follow was due, I believe, in large part to the ground work that had been laid by Tom and in the many open and direct conversations that we had about his eventual death. Without these sorts of conversations, the questions are often not asked, possibilities not discussed and opportunities can be lost. It is much easier, in my experience, as both a physician and a wife, to come to these big decisions gradually, going through a process of exploration and discussion, reflection and decision. And this is hard to do when the topic is never raised.

Chapter Thirteen

． ． ． ● ● ● ． ． ．

So, two days later, after eleven long days in the hospital, we were headed home again—grateful to be back in our bed, in our house, in front of the fire again. And then the next chapter began. Two days after getting back home, we had our initial hospice consultation. Palliative care and Hospice were part of a continuum; it was the same team of physicians and nurses who provided that care, it was a matter of patient choice and condition as to which service was needed. Our first meeting was with the nurse and social worker who came as a team to meet us and begin the long intake process. It felt so odd to sit at our dining room table with people we had just met and talk about end of life and terminal care for Charles, who was sitting there, leading the conversation.

Once again, he was clear in stating his wishes, "I am not interested in heroics and don't want to be resuscitated. I am not ready to stop all treatments, and I don't really feel as if I am dying right now."

"Yes," the nurse answered. "You are the one in charge here; the decisions are yours to make."

"Our job is to help you be able to stay at home and to care for you here if at all possible, if that is what you want."

"We can leave this DNR form that Tom has signed and that directs emergency personnel, if called, that you are not to be resuscitated. This form needs to be kept on the refrigerator door, that is where they know to look for it."

"OK," Charles answered. "That sounds reasonable and I will sign it now."

The conversation continued for a while, with Charles answering questions about his medical history, his current symptoms, his goals for this next phase of his life.

"I want to be at home, with Martha and Conor, and Sean and Colin when possible. I would like not to be in pain. But I am not ready to give up the ghost, and I want to still be able to live my life." *So typical of Charles,* I thought, *to be almost joking, talking about giving up the ghost.* He wasn't afraid, and wasn't afraid to talk in very direct terms ether.

Even though I was right there at the table, it didn't seem real to me. Perhaps I didn't want it to. Overall, it didn't really feel as if becoming a Hospice patient meant that anything was very different, until the next day. Charles again started to develop leg pain, just three days after leaving the hospital. And this was the moment when I realized that we were truly in hospice care. We called the hospice nurse; we didn't go to the ER.

Susan, the hospice nurse we had met just two days prior, came to visit, and then under Tom's direction, and as previously planned during the intake session, pain medicines were started and we decided to wait this out at home and see how it went. I called Rich to notify him, and he seemed surprised and almost angry about the decision, which upset me. I wanted his support for us in this process, and was grateful when he called me back the following morning to check on Charles and to tell me that he supported whatever Charles decided.

What, I wondered, *would be the new rhythm?* What was "Life in Hospice Care" like? What would be our new normal? These were the questions in my mind as I went to sleep that night, wondering if we were doing the right thing, knowing that some of these decisions would send us in directions or down paths from which there would be no turning back;

some decisions now truly were irrevocable. It wasn't actually that that the decision was irrevocable, because one can change one's mind about being in Hospice care, rather that the consequences of a given decision could be such that some options had been removed. By making the choice to stay at home and treat Charles' leg pain as opposed to going back to the hospital and possibly undergoing another procedure to open up the blood vessel again, it is possible that enough damage could have been done so that another procedure would no longer have been possible, even if he had in fact, changed his mind.

Charles, however, seemed confident in his decision and sufficiently comfortable with the current plan. That first weekend home, Russ McDow came by the house to check on him and to look at the leg. He was completely supportive of the plan to stay at home and watch it, which helped both of us. Charles was getting pain medicine pretty regularly, and he seemed both to tolerate that well and to have good pain relief, so we were able to relax a bit, into the weekend.

My brother Rob arrived on Saturday; he drove down from Rochester just to be with us; it was a wonderful gift. He was my "big brother"; I needed to lean on him, and was grateful that he was there. He and Charles and Conor and I had a good weekend together. Charles slept a great deal of the time, but Rob and Conor and I cooked and talked and just hung out by the fire until he left on Sunday. It was hard to see him go, but I knew that he was there for me and would be.

And then we did settle into "life under Hospice care." The new routine was soon established; it consisted of my going to my office, Charles occasionally still coming with me sometimes for a couple of hours in the morning, and our time together at home. We would have our breakfast coffee time together, as we always did, and have some time to talk. Most days, I would come home at noon for lunch, and by then, he would be up from a nap and join me for a bit. Often, Conor came by at lunchtime just to check in and talk. In the afternoons, Charles usually slept, and by the time I got home, he would be ready to come downstairs and be with me by the fire. Some days he was able to stay up longer in the day and be at the computer or read, but his ability to do either of those was diminishing.

Our evening times were sacred for us. We would sit in front of the fire, have a drink and eat some food and talk ... we talked for hours; about our fears, out love, our joys, our hopes. We often talked about the fact that we knew that he was dying, and what that meant. We cried, we laughed, we held each other ... we spoke of our dreams and the future. And we gave each other our love, our presence and our hearts. We knew that we were there "to go the distance" together, as we had always been.

One of my great struggles was having to realize and accept that in fact, I couldn't "go the distance" with him. I often said that I would gladly do this for him, which I knew that I couldn't. I wasn't the one dying. He would have to do that last part by himself. We had always tried so hard to stay together, to stay in sync, in each of these crises. And now, in this most critical of crises, I knew that the time would come when I could no longer accompany him, when I would have to let go and he would have to take the final part of the journey alone. My hope and my prayer for him was that when that time came, that the light and love from the other side would be so strong and welcoming that he would be able to cross without resistance.

On several occasions in the weeks that followed, I had the distinct sense of the presence of both his mother and grandmother; each long dead. I had never met either of them, but felt deeply that I knew them on some deeper, energetic level. Each time I was aware of their presence, it was a peaceful, loving feeling that I experienced, and although I couldn't fully rationalize it, I felt certain that it was significant and found myself hoping that he might eventually feel this too.

Chapter Fourteen

February was rich for us; full of intense time with family and close friends. There was an underlying sense of poignancy, each of us fully aware of the tenuousness of our time together, but we also celebrated. We celebrated by spending time, all of us, here, in our house, with the fire, music, good food and drinks. Sean and his daughter Becca came back the first weekend in the month, along with Patrick, Conor's best friend since second grade. Patrick had long been a part of our family, and not only were he and Conor close, he and Charles were very close as well. They loved each other.

That Saturday evening, we cooked a big dinner and as we all sat down in the dining room to eat, I raised my glass to toast Charles and all of us and Patrick burst into tears. There was no hiding the fact that we all knew we wouldn't have many more of these evenings together; but we chose to continue to live life as fully as possible for as long as we could.

Later that evening, after Charles had gone to bed, the rest of us sat in front of the fire, listened to music, drank wine and talked. There were a bunch of us, Sean and Becca, Patrick and Conor, my friend Susan and myself, talking about everything. It was sometime after 10 when Charles came back downstairs, empty drink glass in his hand, only partially clothed in his tee shirt and underwear. He seemed confused by us all being here;

he didn't quite recall that we had all had dinner together. He joined us for a minute, then got up to refill his drink.

After a few minutes, I walked into the kitchen just in time to see Conor and Patrick, together, getting him into his PJ pants ... and my eyes filled with tears, watching their tenderness with this now quite "old" man whom they both adored. He came back and joined the rest of us for about an hour—enjoying the music and the conversation—before we both went back upstairs and back to bed. The rest of them stayed up till late in the night; I knew they needed that time together to talk and just be together.

Sunday afternoon it rained; it was dark and generally unpleasant outside. Charles had been napping; it was time for Patrick to leave. He came upstairs to see Charles and say goodbye. Looking at this man he had known most of his life, Patrick said, "I love you."

Charles answered "same", and shut his eyes. I imagined that it would be the last thing he would ever say to Patrick. And then I watched Patrick leave, in tears.

And so the weeks went by, with regular visits from the hospice team, piecing together our days, holding on to our times together as best we could. Charles had his first visit to his physician Rich's office since deciding to go with Hospice. I know that I was anxious about the visit, worrying that he would somehow voice disapproval or disagreement with that choice. But Rich didn't, and was actually quite wonderful. There was a question as to why Charles' voice was so weak; it had dramatically changed and he had lost almost all volume. Rich assessed the situation, discussed the possible things that could be causing it, and then proceeded to suggest that we not do a lot of testing if we weren't going to treat anything too aggressively. He suggested that he try some medication for reflux and see if it helped. Charles seemed very amenable to that plan and I was grateful not to have a lot of further testing suggested. Rich ended the visit saying that he fully supported Charles in the choices he was making and that he would be there with him. It was a true gift. Charles trusted and admired Rich, and having his approval was very important.

It was during this time too, that we finally, with the help of our attorney, revised our wills and got all the paperwork we needed in place. We had the Medical Advanced Directive, the durable medical power of attorney, the DNR and the wills, and our attorney also helped us make sure everything we had was shown as jointly owned. He knew this would greatly help me and simplify the estate process, once Charles died. As much as we had procrastinated in getting this task done, it was a relief to have it completed and not have to think about it any longer. These forms can seem daunting both because of the detail involved but also because of the emotions inherent in making the decisions, but they are absolutely essential to have in place, and the relief of having them done was huge. I knew that we should never have waited as long as we did to complete them.

Since coming home from the hospital, Charles had been losing a great deal of weight and he was developing increasing nausea. It was a concern and no one had a good explanation as to why. Perhaps his medication, perhaps the disease, perhaps bowel ischemia, perhaps angina, perhaps the colon cancer had returned. His wasn't eating much at all, and was on occasion, vomiting. He was down almost twenty pounds; it was alarming. Charles had started to say, "Something is wrong."

We talked about different things that could be done to see what was going on, such as blood work, scans and other tests, because Charles thought that he would want to know what was wrong, even if he continued to choose not to treat it. I know that I was looking for some understanding of what I was seeing and to try to get a sense of what it meant. We were both confused by these symptoms. There was so much uncertainty in our lives, that the thought of having a definitive answer sounded appealing to me and to us. In discussing the options available, the Hospice nurse said repeatedly to him, "You're in charge here; you make the decisions. We will follow your lead."

It was true that over the years I would often follow Charles' lead, and now, in this most difficult of situations, we would all take his lead. I felt the tears well up, remembering when I had first heard his strong confident voice … at 16 years old. No wonder I took his lead, and no wonder that I wanted so desperately to continue to do so…

The weight loss and nausea continued; Rich called to check on him and suggested that he get blood work done to see if that would shed any light on what was going on.

When Charles and I discussed that, he said that he would probably choose to do chemo again if this was a cancer recurrence; that he would back out of Hospice and go for treatment if that were the situation. I was initially surprised by that, because it seemed like such a shift in his thinking, but understood it better after reflecting on it a bit, and I had to remember that it was all speculation at this point and that what was important was to stay present in the moment. I tried to focus on where we were right then, and to understand that it would unfold as it would and that we would deal with whatever it was that came up. We didn't do anything just yet; we waited.

On her next visit, the Hospice nurse was alarmed by his ongoing weight loss, and she arranged for Tom to make a visit. Tom, the Hospice doctor, was the one now who was mostly in charge of the day to day concerns. At the house again, Tom was masterful in how he approached and handled the situation. He discussed the list of possibilities and discussed testing that could be done. He was clear that there were and would be decisions to be made, and that some of those decisions would pull Charles back out of Hospice care, even if just for a while. He put no judgment into his words, just stated the facts. Charles was able to say that he wasn't at all sure that he would be opposed to further testing and even treatment; he needed to think it over.

Finally, Tom said, "You, Charles, are the only one who can make the decisions. But you need to understand that you need to decide fairly soon, because there are some decisions that are time sensitive."

This was another occasion when I was able to witness what I had come to see as the "sacred dance" of a beautiful physician-patient encounter. Tom was skilled at guiding the conversation, teasing out the information that he needed to know, being clear in what he saw as possibilities, being non-judgmental, deferring to Charles in terms of the choices and decisions to be made. At the end of the conversation, Tom pulled his chair over close to Charles and examined him while sitting in the chair at the dining room table. Just watching him take his hand and measure his pulse was beautiful—he was gentle and yet strong and treated him with an almost reverence. This was a human being in the midst of the most difficult of journeys, and Tom took his time, gave him his attention and his respect. It brought tears to my eyes to watch.

In the end, the blood work didn't shed any light on the situation, and Tom felt strongly that the normal lab results argued against a cancer recurrence. There was still the option to do scans, but Charles elected to see what a bit more time would bring. His medications were adjusted, and we waited.

He had some good days and some bad days in the couple of weeks that followed. At worst, he was vomiting frequently; at best, he had mild nausea. The thought was that perhaps it was the medicines; so multiple adjustments were made. Some of the changes seemed to bring relief for a few days, some did not.

One of my concerns was trying to understand where we were in the process, and trying to get a sense of what was likely to happen and when. I told the Hospice team that I was going to need some help with that; and asked for guidance. I knew that any assessment I made was through the eyes of a wife, and that I was not as likely to see the clues as I would have been in working with a patient. I wanted to know if and when they thought that his death was imminent, and wanted to be certain they would talk with me about the changes they were seeing.

"I don't have a clear perspective on his situation, you know," I said to the Hospice nurse. "My vision is pretty clouded right now, and I am losing my objectivity. I want you please to tell me what you are seeing and noticing, and not assume that I am aware of it all. Please…"

She was reassuring when she said, "Of course. I will tell you what I see. But you do know that we never know for sure…"

"Yes, I do know that," I answered. "But knowing you will be direct with me will help me a lot. Thank you."

The back and forth nature of Charles' situation was challenging. It wasn't a straight trajectory, and although I knew that to be the likely course, I found it hard. Sometimes it seemed we were nearing the end, then later that same day, he would be feeling well enough to be in his chair by the fire and talking. What I couldn't see clearly at the time was that the peaks and valleys were getting closer together and less dramatic in either direction.

At one point, in all the discussions about the weight loss and trying to understand what was going on, I asked Tom if this situation surprised him. All through the past year, with each event and prolonged recovery, we had been encouraged; people telling Charles that he was "doing great". And that other than our decision to go with Palliative/Hospice Care, nothing really had changed.

And yet, everything had changed. To me, his symptoms seemed to be in need of an explanation. I felt as if I was watching a ping-pong match; it felt to me that there had to be another explanation for what we were witnessing, that there must be another process going on because his symptoms were changing. My paradigm in medicine was to try to understand symptoms, determine the cause and find the treatment. And yes, we had chosen to go with Hospice so the paradigm itself was changed. But I still felt that I wanted to understand.

Tom's response was one of those moments when the stark reality of what we were dealing with hit me hard. He said, "No, Martha, it doesn't surprise me. We see this." He described the situation as a sort of "piling on", the culmination of all that Charles had been through in the prior year.

"I see the last hospitalization as perhaps the event that tipped the scale and changed the balance."

And then I understood. He was, slowly, and although perhaps on an unpredictable trajectory, dying. I didn't know how it would unfold; we didn't know. I felt sad and almost lost. I wanted desperately to hold on— to him, to us, to our life together. But it was suddenly more clear to me and I knew I was losing him. Now I had to focus on the how, the process. No longer the what.

Charles and I discussed it all again that evening—in particular, the process of deciding when one had had enough and deciding to go with palliative care/hospice. He talked about not feeling as if he was there, and then we talked again about his decision to decline the pacemaker which seemed to mean that he was partly there, at least. He agreed, but as we talked, he said, "I don't really feel as if I am dying just yet." We talked about Charles also needing to talk with Tom and his team and letting them know that it was important to both of us that they be direct and honest with us when they saw clear signs of where Charles was and what was happening to him. We both had this need.

I had wanted very much to support Charles and his decision about further testing, but once again, this was a decision that only he could make. I felt that it would become clear to him in the ensuing days as to what to do. As we talked that night, I did thank him for having these incredibly difficult discussions. We both admitted through our tears, that we were okay sharing our fears with each other; something for which I will be forever grateful.

In my journal, I tried to capture my shifting thoughts and feelings. "It is so hard to understand all of this; I know he's dying, and yet I am not sure. Maybe I don't want to be sure. But I know I don't want to "miss it." I want to know what Tom and the team see that makes them know it's getting close. And I want to be with Charles through this process; and be there as his wife. I know I am still a doctor, but I am more of a wife here, and less a doctor.

It's odd—initially the choice of hospice seemed a great way to stay out of the hospital and to be able to get care for the bad leg at home. The full realization of the fact that it means you're in the dying process is easy to miss, particularly as daily life goes on. My brain knows, my heart and soul don't want to admit it. Any yet, I don't want to deny it and risk not being fully present for Charles and for the experience. My head is spinning, my heart is breaking and I want to cry."

I kept thinking, and hoping, that Charles would get better again; that he would get back to more of himself and that we would get back to our life together. I knew that the sphere of our lives had been significantly diminished, but it was still our life, and I was desperate for it to return. In the past, in all the many health crises he had experienced, he had always rallied and managed eventually, to get better. Part of me was quite certain that he would again, this time too, and really most of me knew that he wouldn't. Deep down inside, I knew that he was in fact dying, and I knew that he knew it too. Even so, we each continued on as if perhaps it might not be so … for just a little longer … perhaps….

And then one day in mid-February, he seemed to know very clearly the point we had reached. He was definitely dying. As we lay in our bed and held each other and wept and talked, he said that he didn't think there was anything we could do about what was going on, that we would just hold each other and get through it the best we could. We had finally admitted it to ourselves and to each other.

I went back and forth between wanting to know what would happen and when, and then not wanting to put my energy into that, knowing full well that what was going to happen would happen regardless. I didn't want to spend my time thinking about the future; I wanted to stay present in the moment, feeling very strongly that we were running out of time. And later that weekend, we talked about seeds for the garden that summer and planned what to order.

Charles was not in denial during this time. He clearly understood what was happening and he knew where he was headed. He chose to keep a positive outlook and to hope for a different or better outcome; despite understanding that it wasn't likely to occur. What I witnessed in him was the balance between hope and understanding reality. These are not opposites, and it's not a zero-sum game. We can hold both, hope and truth. I remembered the family meeting at Christmas time when Charles talked about his death. "We all know it's coming," he said. "I hope it's not soon."

It made me reflect on my medical training, and the inherent conflict I had seen. Physicians sometimes think that talking with a patient about their prognosis and being honest and direct might remove the possibility of hope, thereby possibly provoking a patient to give up. We were taught to hold out hope at all costs, even, it seemed, at the cost of not being fully direct. It seems to me, however, that one can always maintain hope; knowing and understanding facts doesn't detract from that. And furthermore, it is not up to the physician to decide what information the patient should know, it is up to the physician to help the patient understand and deal with the information.

I watched Charles navigate these waters; watched him understand that he was dying and witnessed his hope that it wouldn't be soon, that something might happen to change the course of things. It was a dance, back and forth, over and over again, gradually moving ever closer to acceptance and, hopefully, peace with the inevitable.

And so we arrived at the place where I now knew Charles was fully aware of the truth of his situation, and he was able to choose how he approached and traversed the experience. It was his life and his death, and his choices as to how he lived his death were his to make. I was grateful for his and our awareness. I am not sure that everyone is afforded similar awareness, and I would imagine that not knowing and understanding, and perhaps being confused about it might make it more difficult. What I do know is that our long, drawn out process of discussions helped him, and us, be at this place of awareness, and I deeply believe that his and our approach to dealing with his anticipated death honestly, directly and openly was instrumental in creating a richness to the experience that helped us all.

Chapter Fifteen

· · ● ● ● · ·

Over the next few days, Charles' nausea returned and he developed a new shortness of breath. He had been at home under hospice care for about three weeks, and this was a new development. Susan, the hospice nurse, came for a visit and was a bit alarmed by the change; she ordered oxygen to be delivered later that day.

When I walked her out to her car, I asked her what she thought, and she said that she "always pays attention to changes". I understood this to mean that she thought she had seen a significant change in Charles, and that was important. I had wanted to ask because Colin was planning a visit for early March, about two weeks out, and I was beginning to wonder if we should move that up. Susan thought that might be a good idea. She encouraged me to do what I felt in my gut. Susan also witnessed Charles being confused that day, which alarmed her. He had been having some intermittent confusion; sometimes he was perfectly clear, and at other times much less so. On this day, it was very obvious. He wasn't clear, and he wasn't making a lot of sense in what he said. Perhaps that was because of his shortness of breath and a lack of oxygen, perhaps something else. But it was a shift and warranted attention.

As I returned to the house, I wondered what experiencing confusion was like for Charles, and what he was thinking. I wondered if he was thinking a lot about dying. From episodes he would tell me about, I knew that he was continuing to have his experiences in "the other dimension". These always occurred at night, and I would wake to hear him talking to someone I couldn't see or hear. He was increasingly comfortable with these experiences and described the people as somewhat familiar, although not fully identifiable to him. And this is where the doctor in me had to give space to the woman who had to allow for phenomenon that was not measurable by scientific instrumentation. I deeply believed that not only was he witnessing the other world, but I found myself with the sense that he was truly in both worlds at those times; a foot on each side.

Tom came by later that day, after the hospice nurse had called him with her concern about the changes she had seen in Charles. He and I talked after he had seen Charles and made some medication adjustments. Tom asked me, "Has Charles been saying anything different to you?"

"Yes," I admitted. "He told me that he doesn't think there is anything much more for us to do."

Tom looked at me at that point and said, "Do you know what you are going to do when you walk in here one evening and he is gone?"

"I know what I wouldn't do," I answered.

"My suggestion would be just to get in the bed with him and be there with him for a while."

Tom's honesty and directness were in fact, a relief to me, and the words were so painful to hear. But I knew that he was and would continue to be honest. So finally, I asked him…. I told him that I, like Charles, had gone into this really thinking that it was about caring for the foot, and that I hadn't really thought that he was dying, but that now it seemed that he was, to which he answered, "Yes."

I asked if he thought it would be OK to wait the two weeks for Colin to get here, to which he suggested we assess that by asking Colin how important it was for him to see Charles before he died, and that if it would be awful if he didn't, to come now. However, he also told me that he didn't think that it would be that soon, and that before that, he would first get weaker, spend more time in bed and eventually not be able to get up out of bed. He agreed to let me know when he thought that we were getting close. He also asked me to think about whether Charles wanted to be in bed upstairs or downstairs. He told me that he thought we should expect him to get more confused, restless and agitated, and that they would be giving us additional medications to help with that.

It was an enormous relief, finally, to have had the conversation and to feel a clearer sense of where we were, and it was gut wrenchingly sad. And I was aware of the fact that in my normal world, I would be discussing all of this with my Charles ... and that I couldn't do that now. I felt as if the loss had already begun.

Following Tom's advice, Conor, Colin and I had a conference call the next day to talk about Colin's planned trip out here from Seattle. We told him what Tom had said and he decided to move his trip up. He arrived two days later and spent the next ten or so days here. Mostly, they were good days for Charles. He slept a great deal, but when he was up, he was generally alert and able to participate in whatever we were doing, albeit for short intervals. Colin took over the job of managing his medications, which was both helpful for me and, I believed, good for him. There were lots of nice hours of sitting by the fire together.

The next week, Sean came to visit. I think that he, Colin and Conor wanted to be at home with Charles together, and I know it meant the world to Charles. He had always loved having the three of them together; this time would be no different. It was expectedly bittersweet, but the experience was rich and one to be treasured. In the evenings, Conor usually cooked and the rest of us would keep Charles company by the fire. No longer actively participating in the conversations quite as he used to, Charles nonetheless listened and sometimes, even commented. He would doze off frequently, and always smiled when he woke and found us all still around him, music playing, drinks flowing and food cooking. We were together, we laughed, cooked and ate, drank and talked; there were tears shed too.

As I looked around at us all those days, it was so apparent—everyone knew what was happening. And despite that, everyone chose to continue to celebrate life as long as we had Charles still with us. When the time came, it was hard to see Colin go, and hard, I know for him to leave. But he had been able to be here while Charles was still actually present, and that was what was important to him and to all of us.

Shortly before Colin's visit, I realized that I needed someone to talk to; someone to help me in this process. I wanted to talk with my priest. But unfortunately, I didn't have a relationship with the priest at the church I had attended over the years. I had in the past, but with a major leadership change in that church, I no longer felt particularly connected there, and had not yet found a replacement church.

I was born and brought up a Catholic, so focusing on finding a priest to talk to seemed like the right thing to do. When I mentioned to Charles that I felt this need one evening, he reminded me how much I had liked working with an Episcopal priest in our town, John Ohmer. He was right. The year before, when a patient and a friend of mine was dying, I'd met John and found him to be both honest and direct.

John was the Priest at St James, the Episcopal Church in Leesburg. Charles had been brought up an Episcopalian, and although we had occasionally attended an Episcopalian church, Charles was not at all religious; in fact, he abhorred "organized religion". But it had been an important part of his life growing up, and as with me and my connection to the Catholic Church, there were parts of the service that were still very meaningful to him. One of his favorites was the *Nunc Dimittis* in the Evening Song Service. This had always spoken to him, and it was something he dearly loved.

When I called John, and asked if we could meet, he graciously agreed. And when I went to meet him in his office, I was very aware that I was not a member of his congregation, nor even his denomination. I wasn't sure that I should be asking for his help. Yet he welcomed me warmly. I told him what was happening and that I needed help. I told him that I was struggling with some of the big life and death questions, and that I didn't want to do this alone.

"Martha," he kindly said. "I am happy to offer you help and support, however I can. Let me begin by offering you this church for Charles' funeral if you would like that. And I am happy to have you feel free to attend the church for your own support and nourishment. Don't feel pressured to join, just come and take what you need at this time. There is no need for you to do more than that."

I was overwhelmed by his generosity and his kindness. He also told me that he had a number of books on the dying experience and that he would look for some of those and bring them to me. Lastly, he offered to come meet with Charles and Conor, and to talk with them, if that would be helpful.

I left there feeling a great sense of relief, relief that I, in fact, wasn't going to have to do this alone, and relief that there was a connection to the Divine that I felt I really needed and wanted and hadn't been able to find. Although no longer very actively practicing my catholic religion, the Church had always been a place of refuge for me in times of crisis. I had often found it hard to pray in times of stress, but knew that feeling the connection was important to me. Having John's generous offer to support me and guide me was an enormous gift. I knew now that I would be supported in that dimension of the experience, and relieved to have some spiritual structure to the process.

When I talked it over with Charles, he said that he would be happy to meet with John, and so I arranged for them to meet the following week.

John met with the three of us; Charles, Conor and me. He came to the house and the four of us sat in the living room, in front of the fire. The meeting was informal, and he was warm and kind and offered support to all of us. He talked with Charles about his upbringing in the Episcopalian church in New Orleans, and they shared stories about some mutual acquaintances. He was gentle and kind, and did not at all sound judgmental. As he talked, he talked about wanting to be a support for us in this process, and then he said to Charles, "What are your thoughts about a funeral, Charles? What can I do to help with that"?

After a minute of hesitation, Charles answered, "I don't much care, really. I never wanted to have a funeral. But," he added, looking at John, "I've come to realize that a funeral would be important to Martha and Conor. So, I guess I don't object to the idea." John smiled gently. "I understand that you don't care now. And you probably won't care when the time comes either. I expect you'll be in such a state of bliss then it won't matter." Charles smiled a small, understanding smile.

"But," John continued, "I think it might help you now to know that I'll help arrange for a funeral that will support Conor and Martha when the time comes."

"Yes, I get that," Charles answered. "And I am OK with it. Thank you."

I wondered at the time if he was thinking about his trips to the "other side", and what he might be seeing. The conversation didn't seem to upset him at all. Nor did it seem to disturb Conor; I think he and I each felt relief for the support of John. I know I felt enormous relief that I wasn't going to need to plan a funeral that I knew I would need and that Charles would not have wanted. John had provided for me; and I believe for Charles, a spiritual dimension to the process without a layering of Religion. This felt in alignment with what was important to each of us; it felt authentic.

Conor and Charles each said afterwards that they liked him and felt comfortable with him and would be happy to meet and talk again.

That night, long after John was gone and house was silent, I lay in bed next to Charles, feeling a tremendous relief because I now knew that I would have additional support for my own as well as Charles' needs … as the end approached. And once again, I was so very thankful that we could be open and honest and direct in discussing these most difficult of subjects, and feeling my heart being torn out with sadness. The pattern didn't change; this was a journey of juxtapositions and opposites being held as simultaneously true, over and over again. Gratitude and sorrow, hope and fear, love and sadness—all of it.

In the days that followed, my thoughts were all over the place. I would find myself wondering what was happening, as if I didn't know. Sometimes, in the midst of cooking dinner or doing laundry, I found myself feeling as if things would in fact, get better again. Perhaps, I hoped. We could go on like this for a while … we could be OK.… And then, an hour later, I would be thinking about funerals and the sadness would wash over me like a wave.

Sometimes, I would have this momentary thought that he wasn't dying and that he would get better, at least somewhat, and that our lives would continue on as they were.

Some days, he was still able to be downstairs and eat a small amount. He sat at the table and by the fire, enjoying being up and around. Occasionally, he would be on his computer, but that was rare. I would look at him and think that he was in fact "fine" knowing full well he wasn't. The reality was that his being "fine" was for short bursts of time, inside that very small sphere that our lives had become. By any other comparison, it was a very small sphere of existence.

Charles was now, intermittently talking more about death too. One morning, after a night where he had again been talking in his sleep a lot, he told me, "You were talking a lot in your sleep, too."

"Maybe we were talking to each other in the ether," I responded tentatively. Charles responded, "Maybe we were practicing or getting ready.…"

Lying in bed one night, I asked Charles again about his experience in "the other dimension".

"What is it like?" I asked. "What do you think about it? Is it scary?"

Just as he had before, he replied, "It doesn't feel new to me. And it isn't unpleasant. I generally don't recognize people or places, but somehow it feels familiar and comfortable." I found it fascinating; it felt to me as if he had a foot in the other world and that he was "trying it out" before he decided to cross over.

I sensed that Charles was now trying to separate a bit. There was nothing tangible, it was an intuitive sense that I had. I knew that in the end, it was he who was going to have to do the leaving. I knew too, that I would have to try to provide him help in that process, by telling him, when the time came, that it was OK. I had seen this happen many times; a dying person sometimes seems to wait for permission from a loved one to go. I felt myself getting closer to where I felt I could do this for him, for us.

As the days went on, any illusions about a miraculous turn-around vanished, Charles continued to get weaker and his pain got worse. Some days he spent mostly in bed, others he seemed restless and was up a lot. He had trouble sleeping some of the time; at other times, he wanted to talk about making plans for the future. For me, it was like a rollercoaster ride; the ups and downs were challenging. I felt as if I were riding the tail of a dragon.

I spent many of my nights awake and thinking about what was occurring; sometimes wondering what he was thinking about and reflecting on the whole process; how we had gotten to this place and where we were headed. Wondering how I would survive without him, knowing that I would have to, wondering how the kids would be and worrying about the future. And at the same time, trying to hold on to memories and the love that was still present and palpable. I marveled at how Charles was acting with such incredible dignity and grace. He never complained about his condition. He would get upset about it when we talked about it on occasion; it wasn't as if he were in denial. It was just that regardless of what was happening to him, he moved forward and onward anyway; he was being Charles. That had long been the "Charles Way"—just to move forward, come what may. It was this same attitude that had been challenging for me at times like after a heart attack or hospitalization for his colon cancer. He would try to carry on as if nothing had happened, making the adjustments he needed, acknowledging the reality but not talking a lot about the experience. It was both challenging and admirable; it was Charles.

By mid-March, the hospice team was getting increasingly concerned about Charles' diminished physical stamina; he was still getting around without using the walker that was ready for him to use at home, or the cane, but he wasn't always very steady on his feet. Most of the time, he was not using his oxygen, and he was intermittently not always clear-headed. I knew that I had to think about not leaving him alone; I also knew that I wasn't ready to hire people to be with him all day, and knew that he would be very resistant to that idea. It simply wasn't possible for Conor and/or me always to be home, so we had to have a backup plan.

Several of our friends had been offering to help for some time. I began to take them up on their offers, asking a number of people to stop by during the day to see if Charles needed anything, to walk the dog and so forth. That felt more natural to me and didn't seem to bother him. My mother was planning a visit the next week, and then my sister Sara was planning to come again, this time for a long weekend. Having them here with us would mean that I had fewer outside visits to arrange.

And then one evening, when I came home from work, there was a large bag of peanuts on the kitchen counter. Charles was in the chair by the fire. I assumed that someone who had stopped by brought them. Charles got up and came into the kitchen looking sheepish. I didn't understand, but he said: "I goofed; I forgot about not being allowed to drive, got in the car and drove to the grocery store and bought peanuts."

I burst out laughing, and was shocked at the same time.... He had gone to the store in his PJs, by some fluke had some money in the pocket of his fleece jacket, hadn't gotten stopped, hadn't had an accident or gotten lost, and was back home and safe!

Unbelievable, really... I think that he was surprised, a bit unnerved by it and also secretly proud that he did it so well. I struggled a bit with the decision, but knew that I had to take the keys from him. It was something that I never wanted to have to do ... but he was on too much medication to risk his getting behind the wheel again.

A few days later, I saw Tom at the Family Medicine department meeting at the hospital and talked with him about the challenge of seeing Charles go back and forth between being seemingly "fine" and then not fine at all, not even really being aware. It was as if he would rally for a bit, especially if any visitors were here, and then his energy gave out and he was not able to stay focused and present. He would be restless, wandering, looking and reaching for things ... not being at all clear.

I said to Tom, "It's so hard to see him this way, and it's hard not to ride the wave of hopefulness when he has moments of seeming to be fine."

And he answered, "That is all part of the dying process, Martha. I have to tell you— you should expect that the times of confusion and loss of clarity will become more frequent and longer. Charles will get weaker and weaker, and eventually won't be able to get out of bed. You should decide, soon, if he is going to be upstairs or downstairs when that happens. I say soon, because the change will happen overnight."

Chapter Sixteen

* * ● ● ● ● * *

I was grateful for the directness with which Tom spoke to me, and it reminded me again of the reality. Had I been working with a patient, I am sure that I, too, could have seen where we were, but my longing to have it not be so was clearly obstructing my view.

After talking with Tom, and being able to acknowledge again to myself that Charles actually was actively dying, I knew that I wanted to shift into a place of really paying attention to and being present with the experience. I didn't want to deny it. I didn't want to write off things that happened as coincidence or serendipity. I wanted to be present with him as we navigated this part of the journey together. It would have been easy, I was afraid, to get lost in the details of the day, the business of all that needed to be done and managed, and not to be present in the time that we had. I wanted to see and experience the process in its entirety.

My mother back came as planned, and spent a week with us, giving me the ability to be in the office some during the days and to worry less about Charles being in the house alone. Charles was getting weaker, and had started dropping the match as he tried to light his pipe. Those hands that I loved; those hands that had made furniture, cleared dead trees, tilled our garden, carried sheets of plywood, held me … were now unable to hold the pipe or a lighted match. Bit by bit, the man I loved and had chosen to spend my life with, was disappearing in front of my eyes. I got some lighters for him and though I really didn't want to keep taking things away from him ... I put the matches away. At least when you let go of a lighter, the flame goes out.

After my mother left, my sister Sara came again for a visit. She had been there for me time and time again; and I leaned on her a lot. Those days that she was here, Charles seemed pretty good. But then he started to develop more pain, nausea, and he was vomiting. In fact, for weeks now, he kept his stainless-steel bowl with him at all times. Charles carried it with him as he went from room to room; it just became part of the routine. You forget, or don't allow yourself to acknowledge, how not normal that is ... but it was normal for us. Often now, he was miserable. Never sure as to why he was vomiting, we tried multiple med changes, and eventually the vomiting lessened.

The pain continued, though, and his restlessness as well. Nights seemed to be the most challenging. He spent a lot of the night times awake and up—wandering, holding onto the furniture or the wall when he was unsteady. He would turn the lights on and off; take a shower sometimes, and wake me to ask about something. He seemed to have no idea that it was the middle of the night. This was sad and painful to witness.

Charles' intermittent disorientation was one of the hardest aspects for me. He had always enjoyed a razor-sharp mind, a vast base of knowledge and a photographic memory. To see that vanish and for him not to be sure of where he was, was a deeply disturbing experience. It wasn't just the body that I was watching disappear, it was his mind as well. I only hoped that he was not so aware of his confusion; it would have distressed him greatly.

Periodically, John Ohmer would come by and talk with him; the Hospice people were in and out, and friends too, were in and out. Conor was here every day, as he had been the entire year. He gave Charles, and us, the gift of his presence—the greatest gift he could have given. I loved to see the smile on Charles' face every time that Conor walked in the back door.

Sometimes during these days and weeks, Charles seemed to be clear and almost fine, but the times when he wasn't fine were increasing. His stamina was fading, his physical body was fading, his ability to stay present and focused were fading. It was an increasingly rapid decline that seemed to be taking on a life of its own—like a snowball rolling downhill—picking up speed as it goes. The times that I had "my Charles" were getting fewer and farther apart; I was already losing him despite desperately wanting to hold on. More and more each day, I felt him slipping through my fingers.

In late March, our dear friend, Susan Barr, came to visit. We had met Susan almost thirty years earlier, when she had been Charles' nurse in the ICU at Georgetown when he had had his first heart attack, even before we were married. The three of us became friends then, and had remained close friends since. She visited us at least once a year, and she adored Charles. Always one to participate in whatever you were doing, she came both to visit and to help. I know that she wanted to see him one more time.

She left two days later, on a Thursday at the end of March. It was a sad goodbye, knowing it was likely the last she would see him. I was home for the day. I was tired, as was Charles. He, and therefore we, had been up most of the night; he seemed to be having pain. He was restless, wandering and confused. As he had other nights, he turned the lights on and off repeatedly, and told me that he had to get to the basement and turn all the lights off. I was struck by the metaphor, and I was sure that his statements held meaning and significance. I was reminded of the examples of the phenomenon of Near Death Awareness I had read about and how often there seemed to be metaphor for people as they came increasingly close to dying. Was that what turning the lights out meant for Charles? I didn't know for sure, but I thought it probably was.

What was this process of dying like, I wondered repeatedly. *Was there an awareness? Would there be a recognition? A knowing?* Yes, we knew intellectually that Charles was dying; although the when and where and how of it we did not know. But what would it feel like? What would he, and we, be thinking about and experiencing? I searched for guidance from other people's experiences, looked for books on the dying process.

What I found to me to be most interesting and most helpful were writings on what was called "Near Death Awareness". These were descriptions of the actions of people nearing their deaths who communicated in what seemed most like code. There didn't seem to be consensus as to why this occurred, there was nonetheless, a consistency of experience that felt compelling.

People often seemed drawn to talk about travel; plane or train schedules, getting to the airport, bus or train station on time, worrying about where the tickets or the maps were, having their luggage packed. There seemed to be a nearly universal theme of the person being aware that they were going somewhere.

The question remained, and still remains, why the use of metaphor?

As described by Maggie Callanan and Patrick Kelley in their book, *Final Gifts*, "Dying people know they are dying, even if no one else knows or has told them. They attempt to share this information by using symbolic language to indicate preparation for a journey of a change soon to happen."

Their book describes countless stories of patients using metaphor, often of impending travel, to signal their coming deaths.

So when my Charles told me he needed to turn off the lights, or asked me to find him the map, I felt certain he was telling me, this time in code, that he was dying.

And I was grateful to be able to hear and understand, and not to overlook the message with the belief that he was just confused. I wanted to remain alert to those messages. He didn't seem confused to me when he was talking like that; he wasn't particularly grounded in the here and now, but I sensed that he had a strong understanding of what he was saying and doing. It was almost as if he were in the "other dimension" of which he had spoken so many times. And seeing him in this space felt almost otherworldly to me.

We had a hospice visit the day that Susan left, and the nurse saw the change. She ordered a hospital bed to be delivered that day. The time had come they told me, and it signaled a dramatic change in his condition. Clearly, the hospice team felt that he would soon be unable to get in and out of bed easily, and the mechanics of the hospital bed would be helpful. They no longer presented it as a choice to us; they had made the decision. Our only decision was to determine where it was to go, so I moved some things in our back room, and made space for it. It was a small room, with bookshelves, a sofa, chair and a magnificent pine entertainment center that Charles had built. There was a door that opened to the back and onto our terrace, where we sat in the summer. The walls were covered with family photographs. It was a cozy room, but small; yet it did seem the best choice for the bed because the room also opened into the kitchen, clearly the hub of the house; and that meant that even confined to bed, Charles wouldn't be isolated.

When they had ordered the bed, I went to Target to get some sheets, thinking that at least I could make it look nice. Our friend, Karen Blodgett, came by while I was gone, and was there when I came back. She helped me wash the new sheets and we made up the bed that by then had been delivered. It was a hospital bed, so it could be raised and lowered, as could the head of the bed itself., and that made it much easier to get in and out of the bed, and allowed a person to be propped up into a sitting position easily.

I suggested to Charles that we get in that bed to watch a movie that evening; and then go up to our bed for the night. I reminded him that the next day, when I was at work, he would have the choice of whether he wanted to nap upstairs in our bed, or downstairs in this bed.

We, in fact, did watch a movie that night, lying side by side in the hospital bed. And then I lay on the sofa next to him as he slept. He didn't have the energy to go back upstairs.

Chapter Seventeen

. . . ● ● ● . .

The next morning was the first of April. I got up and headed off for work; Charles barely moved. I had been in the office about an hour when I received a call from the hospice nurse Susan, who said, "I'm at the house and I see a profound change in Charles from yesterday to today. I think you should come home." When I arrived home, Charles was still in the downstairs bed; he looked uncomfortable. He was awake, not quite fully present. He was tired, and closed his eyes often. He grimaced some, and didn't communicate much. Susan was adjusting his medicines; and making arrangements for us to have 24-hour nursing care over the weekend. She had determined that we needed the additional assistance, given this change in his status.

I called Conor as soon as I got home to let him know what was going on; he very quietly moved back to the house that day. He and I called Sean and Colin and began to plan for them to come. I talked with my brother Rob and let him know about the change in status.

Sean arrived on Saturday. He had last seen his Dad in early March when he visited and Colin was there. He, Conor and I spent most of the day sitting on the sofa next to the bed where Charles was; all of us together. My friend, Susan Patch, who had been with us during most of the episodes of the prior year, was with us most of that day, helping us with grocery shopping, cooking, walking the dog and holding space for all of us.

Charles would rest some, and then rise to sit up. He wasn't strong enough; however, to stay sitting up, he needed help. One or another of us would sit by him, with him, to help hold him up. He would start to drift off, but then startle back and try to sit up again. Clearly, he wanted to be sitting up, and it was obvious that he couldn't do it himself. It was painful to watch; I ended up sitting for hours behind him in the bed, holding him up and letting him lean back on me. I wasn't sure why he wanted so much to sit up, but it was clear that he did.

Saturday evening, my brother Rob arrived. Once again, he had driven from Rochester to be with us. I will never forget his arrival; he came into the room and sat down on the sofa. Charles opened his eyes and looked at him and said, "Oh, you're here. Does that mean I am that close?"

Rob didn't flinch. He said, "Yes, I am sorry but I think so. Are you ready?" Charles said, "Not yet." Then he closed his eyes again.

Colin was able to get a redeye flight out that night, and arrived at the house on Sunday.

And so we shifted into yet another new routine, of life centered around Charles in the bed in the back room, taking turns sitting with him and being with him. He was dying and yet life was going on all around him; we played music, ate and drank and talked … and waited. I stayed with him, either in the bed with him or on the sofa next to him, staying there at night as well—night after night. I didn't want to leave. And we couldn't leave him alone, he needed help every time he tried to get up and he tried to get up every couple of minutes. We were a small group; Charles, Sean, Colin and Conor and me, Rob, Susan and later Sara. We were with him round the clock; other people came and went, but the core group of us never left for the two weeks that he was in the hospital bed dying. I have often marveled since how we managed to fit; all of us, in this small house and in that small room. The guys are all tall and under normal circumstances I think it would have been stifling. But somehow, the energy expanded the space and there was room … for all of us and for the work that was being done.

Sunday afternoon, Charles wanted to get up and with great effort, walked through the kitchen to the bathroom. I was holding his arm for support as he walked. When he got to the bathroom door, he turned, looked at me and said, "Would you get me the map?" I asked him to repeat himself, not sure if I had understood him. He asked again, and then it hit me and I knew what he was saying; I told him that I would. My spirit knew that this was code for telling me that he was, in fact, dying. My heart was breaking.

My sister Elizabeth arrived that weekend from Chicago to spend some time with us. It had been a long time since she had seen Charles, and it was nice to have her be a part of this with us. We were surrounded by family and friends and having them with us as the process unfolded was a tremendous support for each of us. I was grateful that we were there together as a family, surrounded by friends, each of whom supported us in their own way. I didn't have the bandwidth to do anything more than be present for Charles and to try to support Sean and Colin and Conor. I needed the help of others to keep the house going and lend additional support to each of us as we needed it. We each needed support at different times, and it was a gift. Rob left on Sunday to go back home. I was sure that he didn't think he would see Charles alive again when he left.

Russ McDow came by to check on Charles and to see me, bringing me a book of the *Tao of Dying*, which had been inspirational to him. As he had done in the hospital, Russ just sat with Charles. He didn't try to talk, he just was there.

Nights continued to be a challenge, and having the others present in the house around the clock proved to be helpful. Ours is a very small house. It took some coordination for everyone to find a place to sleep and because I needed help with Charles when he tried to get up at night, Conor and

Colin and Sean ended up taking shifts sleeping so that one of them was always available to help me.

For a couple of days, things were basically unchanged. Charles continued to want to get up often; he was less and less able, and needed more and more help. Tuesday afternoon, I was sitting on the stairs talking with my friend Karen Blodgett, when Conor came to me and said, "Dad wants to go outside."

It was early spring, but still quite chilly out. I told Conor that since there were enough of us to carry him outside, we should do it by all means. We would just need to bundle Charles up first. We put some boots on him, trying not to cause further pain to the leg and foot as we did, slipped his parka on him, and took him outside. He sat out back in the sun, looking at the birds, the trees, the sky. He seemed peacefully immersed in a personal solitude. After a couple of minutes, he was ready to come back inside.

The rhythm of those final days was unique; every morning my friend Peggy showed up with fruit and other breakfast items. She always made sure that the kitchen was cleaned up and she kept track of the food that people were bringing by for us. She was there every evening too, making sure that everyone had what they needed…she was a true gift. The house was continuously filled with people, coming in and out, offering to help, or just to say hi. And all the while Charles lay in the bed in the back room, doing the work of dying.

As the days went on, Charles needed increasingly more help; and each of his three sons took part in helping me take care of their father. It was painful and beautiful to watch. There was so much love in the house, and especially in that room … we were there together as a family and with our friends, and I could see that everyone who was there with us was being changed by the experience. Each was able to experience a sustaining love that was keeping us all afloat. We were united in the common cause of helping usher Charles out of this life and on to the next.

Hospice sent an aide to help me bathe Charles. She was a lovely Indian woman and watching her care for the love of my life brought tears to my eyes; her gentleness and her love and kindness, her compassion was extraordinary. She helped me wash him and change the bed linens without having to get him up, and I was struck by how she treated him with such a combination of compassion and respect. She came several times that week, and kept telling him that she was looking for the dry shampoo for his hair, and that she would find it for him. A simple gift to a dying man. It was beautiful.

Wednesday of that week, there seemed to be a shift. By the late afternoon, Charles seemed different; less present. The energy in the room felt different; there was a palpable sense of anticipation, and his breathing shifted. It had slowed, and there were long pauses between breaths. We all grew increasingly concerned, and began to think that he would die soon. It felt surreal to me; sitting there, watching, waiting ... wondering. Susan called Rob to tell him what was going on. He was back in my house before midnight; how he made that seven-hour drive in that time I will never know; but will be forever grateful to him for it. As he walked in the house, Conor met him at the door and said that he was just in time, it looked as if he were going to die at any minute. We had called John Ohmer, the priest, as he had invited me to do, telling him of the profound change. He was headed over to the house.

A few minutes after midnight John arrived; we were all standing in the back room around the bed, Charles was still breathing but quite erratically. John walked in, came close to the bed, leaned over and said in a full voice,

"Charles, this is John. Martha called me because she thinks you are dying.... Are you going someplace?"

There was a very long pause.... And then Charles pulled himself up, yet again, reached out and shook John's hand. It was, as John described it later, a bone crushing handshake ... and then Charles answered ... in inimitable Charles fashion…, "Ultimately, yes. But not right now." And then he lay back down.…

John stayed for a while, we drank some pear brandy and talked; I think he finally left around 2 am. He told me to feel free to call him at any time if I needed him. I asked him if he really meant that, and he assured me that he did. With a smile, he said that if we were an hour away, he might not have offered. And with that comment, I believed his offer was genuine.

Sara arrived about 4 that morning, having left Boston the evening before when we thought Charles was dying. It was wonderful to have her back.

The next day, we were all sitting in the room with Charles and he was sitting propped up in the bed. He looked at us all and said, "I know that I am supposed to be going somewhere, just not sure where or when. But I need to talk to each of you." And he started going around the circle, saying some words to each of us, basically saying good bye. He paused when he reached the place where Orla, his beloved dog, was lying and said, "Oh I can't talk to you, you're a dog." And then he was back to the beginning of the circle, saying words again to Conor when someone told him that he was repeating himself. Conor quickly said, "I'm OK with getting two turns." Then Charles lay back down, closed his eyes and drifted back off to sleep.

Later that same day, he again seemed confused and asked several of us, "Will someone please tell me what is going on? Are we celebrating a birth?"

It was a lovely and bittersweet analogy; it was Sean who finally spoke, telling him,

"No Dad, we are all here because you are dying. It's not a birth." And Charles seemed to accept that fully, he lay back down and again, drifted back to sleep.

Those two weeks were filled with rich and painful days. John Ohmer showed up repeatedly. Twice he brought Holy Oil with him and anointed Charles and then my hands … "healing hands", he called them. I was so moved watching him anoint my beloved, who was lying not moving in the hospital bed, with the Holy Oil. John blessed him as he anointed him and it was a soothing, healing experience for me. It was truly a gift for me to be able to experience the presence of the Divine in those moments.

The whole atmosphere in the house seemed to be permeated with an awareness that we were in between this world and the next. In this world, the mundane tasks of life were tended to, food was cooked, dishes were washed, and all the while Charles was in the next room on his deathbed inching ever closer to the other world. There was music, and storytelling, and laughter. More than once, I found Rob and Sara teasing each other as they had when we were kids; Rob even shut the basement door on Sara and turned out the lights on her! Every evening we drank pear brandy, which became our signature ritual.

The house was full of an infectious love and light those days. All who were there with us felt it and kept coming back. It was the love that sustained us. It is love, I now know, that is the only thing that really matters. These were the darkest moments of my life and yet the love shined a light that held me and allowed me to go on.

It was interesting those days to watch Orla, our elderly Irish Terrier. She was really Charles' dog; she was completely attached to him, and he to her. She had spent hours on his lap sitting in the chair in front of the fire, especially in the winter months after we came back home from the hospital. So it seemed inevitable that when Charles moved into the bed in the back room, that Orla spent her time on the bed with him. What was interesting was that she was usually near Charles' bad leg, as if she was protecting it. Eventually, as he got worse and the leg got worse, she ended up lying on it.

I kept close to Charles; sitting with him or lying with him, holding on and letting go at the same time. I was increasingly aware of the need to tell him that it would be okay for him to leave that we would all take care of each other and that he didn't have to stay. I knew in my head, and really in my heart, that I needed to do this. And that he needed this, but it broke my heart to say the words.

As I sat or lay next to Charles, I saw him begin to lie on the bed and… just reach.

He would raise his right arm towards the upper right hand corner of the room, towards the ceiling. He did this repeatedly; then his arm would drop back down, he would rest it a bit and then do it again. I had the distinct impression that there was someone he saw there, to whom or for whom he was reaching.

This continued for a full day or two, although it was getting obviously harder for him to raise his arm and reach. I didn't know who was there, but I finally silently asked whoever it was to please, just help him. *Reach out and take him if you have to, because he can't do it alone and I can't do it for him*

I had always known that I would have to "let" him leave, and tell him that it would be all right, and that we would be all right. But this wasn't exactly how I had envisioned that happening.

Late one day, as he was lying with his eyes closed, he smiled the most magnificent smile, and then turned to me and said, quite unexpectedly, "It's more beautiful than you could ever imagine."

Charles was not a religious man, and he was not one to say what he thought you wanted to hear. He was direct and often, brutally frank. To hear him speak these words was a gift; but I know that they were not spoken as a gift. It was what Charles was seeing; he was speaking his truth.

Some might say that people hallucinate when they are in the dying process. And certainly, during Charles' many long illnesses he had times of significant confusion, perhaps hallucinations. At those times, he would be visibly different; he had a vacant look and the things he said generally made no sense. He would often confuse things, weaving bits of one reality with those of another.

But this statement was strikingly different, as had been the times when Charles spoke of being in the "other dimension". There was no blank stare then, no vacant look in his eyes, and no blending of realities. He didn't understand some of what he was experiencing in the "other dimension", but he never expressed concern about the reality of it. He didn't look different; he was most assuredly himself. He had a conviction and an acceptance about it.

So, when he spoke those words to me, I felt no doubt about the reality of it. I knew him well enough to know that he wouldn't really have expected to find such beauty beyond this life; and if he was telling me it was so, then surely, it is so.

I realized then again, that this was the work that Charles was doing; he was teaching me and all of us about the dying process. His process had a purpose that was greater than him leaving this earth plane; ever the teacher throughout his life, he continued teaching to the very end.

And now these words will stay with me forever.

"It's more beautiful than you could ever imagine." They were the last words Charles spoke to me.

Chapter Eighteen

· · ◦ ◉ ◉ ◦ · ·

The group of us who were together for the nearly two weeks that Charles was in bed in the back room, in the final two weeks as he was dying, were each profoundly affected by the experience. Conor, Colin and Sean, Rob, Sara, Susan and I were supported by our friends, by the hospice team – Tom, Susan and Sheila, by our priest, John Ohmer, and by people who couldn't be with us physically but who were with us in spirit. It seemed to me that they too, were affected by the experience; something was happening in that room that is now hard to capture and to articulate. It was the love and the open-heartedness that was compelling—no one wanted to leave. I think that Charles, too didn't want to leave; and that in part, that is why it took such a long time for him to die.

The days were filled with a steady stream of people in and out of the house; there were visits from the hospice team, Peggy was always there morning and evening, friends stopping by. Rob seemed often to be on the phone or his computer; he worked from the dining room table or the living room. Sara, it seemed, did laundry all day long. Sean, Colin and Conor were each present with their Dad the entire time; Susan was in and out throughout the day and with us every evening,

By evening, Rob, and usually Conor were cooking; doing something on the grill right outside the room where Charles was. The smells and the sounds were wonderful. The music was playing and the drinks were flowing. It was a rich, organic, earthy time; the guys would help me tend to Charles, who lay dying as life was going on all around us....

John Ohmer showed up day after day; he even said something once about how he felt drawn to be here with us. We talked, laughed, prayed, ate and drank. Patrick came back for the weekend, and was able to see Charles still alive, one more time. My friends from the medical world, Russ McDow, Stephen Napolitano, Jack Cook, Scott Nagell, all came by to sit with him and to be with us.

Together, we wove a tapestry, thread by thread, that held each of us and sustained us. It was made with love and compassion. It held us, compelled us and supported us, even as my own life was unraveling, a thread at a time.

It was clear to me, as I watched Charles in the dying process, that in the end, all that matters is love. There was such love with us and for him in that process; the love filled the space and held each of us even as the life we were watching was being extinguished.

As the days went on, we started to have more conversations about the specifics; including funeral arrangements. John helped me think of things that needed to be done, calls to make. John and I started talking about plans for a service. Colin began to write an obituary; everyone was getting ready.

One morning, a few days before Charles died, I was sitting at the dining room table, talking with John.

"I want to give you some advice, Martha," he said. "And you need to remember that if you follow this advice, the others in this house will as well, and it is important."

"When Charles dies, I want you to remember not to refer to Charles being at the funeral home, not to talk about them coming to get Charles. He will have died, and all that will be here will be his body. Only his body. It will not be Charles."

"And, don't forget to remove his wedding ring, if you want to … after he is dead and before they take his body."

"I know this may not make a lot of sense to you right now," he said, "but I hope and believe that it will be helpful later."

At that moment, the distinction didn't seem significant to me, but I agreed to try to remember that. I had come to trust John and wanted to try to remember what he said.

And still the vigil continued. The day after the midnight call to and visit from John Ohmer, when Charles announced that he was not going anywhere yet, was the day that he told me "how beautiful it was." Shortly after that, there was another shift, and he became less responsive. His breathing changed; he seemed uncomfortable. That evening, my friend Sheila, a hospice nurse who was not assigned to work with us, came by for a visit at about 11pm. She sat with me, by Charles, all night, watching and trying to get a sense of what was happening. With her there, I actually dozed on and off, on the sofa pushed up against his bed, where I had been the entire week. Charles was not really responsive, but restless. And as dawn came on Friday morning, she said that she was going to call Tom and fill him in.

Friday was a challenging day; everyone was tired and fuses seemed to be getting short. Hospice sent their Chaplin and he administered some Reiki, the thought being that it might help calm Charles some. That afternoon, everyone cleared out of the house for a while, leaving Conor and me alone with Charles and Susan, the hospice nurse, for a couple of hours. The break was good for everyone.

Susan and I were sitting with Charles when she said to him, "Charles, I wish we could see what you can see," and he smiled a huge, gentle smile.

Then she said to him that it was like a river; he could swim against the current and it would be hard, or he could turn on his back, relax and go with the current and it would be easy. I think that he "turned on his back", because I sensed another notch of letting go.

Everyone seemed calmer when they returned to the house in the late afternoon, and Tom came by to check on him. He decided to adjust the medicines again, and when he left that day, he leaned over and said good bye to Charles, telling him that he wouldn't see him again, on this side. On his way out, he told me that he thought that it would be soon.

And then ensued another evening of Rob cooking dinner, everyone sitting around the fire, music playing. Sometime after midnight, as some sat by the fire, some on the sofa next to Charles, we were listening to Willie Nelson, as we had been for the entire week. When a new song started, we all heard Willie sing "Turn out the lights, the party's over." The nervous laughter didn't stop for a long time.

I like to think that somewhere, even if not conscious, Charles enjoyed the laughter, the smells of the food, the music, and knew that we were all there together, with him and for him. I am sure that he did. It is how he would have wanted it. It was the incredible power of love that was sustaining us all.

Saturday was Sara's birthday. Charles was not responsive; the medications had been changed and he seemed to be having seizures almost anytime he was touched. A different nurse came to visit because it was the weekend; she told me we needed to have our clergy come because it wouldn't be long.... She was back on Sunday; nothing had really changed and her message was the same. He was now doing the pre-death breathing called Cheyne stokes; a series of rapid breaths and then long pauses … the hours were long as we waited.

By now it took two of us to turn him, change the sheets, rub his back. Each of Charles sons; large, strong men, so gently and lovingly helped me care for their Dad. Sunday evening, he developed a really high fever; I don't think I have ever touched someone that hot.

The weekend was long and hard, for all of us. Everyone was getting tired; Conor, Sean and Rob were all talking about having to get back to work—no one knew how long this process would go on. My sons teased me that I had called them all home 10 days earlier because his death seemed imminent … and here we still sat.

As a physician, I have worked with families of dying patients and had seen them get to the place where they almost wanted it to be over; and I was seeing that start to happen for us. It isn't death that is wanted, it is for the dying process itself to end. And by the time it was Monday morning and things had shifted yet again, I was seeing this unease as the pervasive emotion in the house. Everyone wanted the process to be over.

Early Monday morning, I noticed another significant change in Charles' breathing; he was now breathing rapidly and shallowly. It was uncomfortable to watch, and I was confused by the shift. I was anxious to talk with hospice about it and to get Tom's thoughts.

The day started badly on several levels. The hot water heater in the house broke; we had no hot water and there were at least six of us in the house. When I called the plumber, and was told they could get to it later in the week, I cut them off, saying, "Let me explain, my husband is dying and I have a house full of people. You have to do this today." Our water heater was fixed within the hour.

It was a bright, sunny and really hot day -- it was about 80; much too hot for that time of year, making it hard to be inside. At least I was able to open the door in the back room and get some fresh air.

And then quite suddenly, Sara had to leave. Her son needed her at home and she pulled out of the driveway about noon; we were both sobbing as she left. I didn't know how much more I could take.... Conor was visibly uncomfortable seeing his father continue to lie in that bed, unable to move, seizing every time he was moved, with nothing changing. Sean was talking about driving back to New Jersey for a day or two to get some work done; Rob had moved into a hotel to have some space to work as well.

Eventually, the hospice nurse came by and once again, they decided to change his medication to see if they could get the seizures to stop. Tom came to visit later that day, and we talked about what options there were in terms of medications. He thought that we should give it overnight and see how he was in the morning before making any other changes.

Everyone seemed to have relaxed again as the day went on; the "routine" was resumed; another evening with music, cooking, story-telling, with me lying in the bed with Charles or sitting beside him, holding his hands, all of us spending time sitting beside him on the sofa.

Chapter Nineteen

⋅ ◦ ⋅ ◉ ◉ ⋅ ◦ ⋅

Early Tuesday morning, Conor and I were the only two up, and we were sitting with Charles, when John Ohmer came by again. He was heading out of town to attend a funeral in Richmond, but wanted to stop by first. He prayed with us, anointed Charles again with holy oil, and then anointed both my hands and Conor's as well. Then he read the *Nunc Dimitts*, the evening song prayer that Charles loved so much. It was a final benediction.

He told me to feel free to call his associate if we needed anything while he was gone; he would be back late that evening or the following day. It was a lovely space in time; both Conor and I felt that it was a special, sacred moment. It seemed to mark a transition, and it felt to me that we had moved into the truly active phase of dying.

Our regular nurse was off that day, so our friend Sheila came in her place.

Together, Shelia and I bathed Charles and in the process, I removed his sock and looked at the foot on his bad leg. It was black … and I knew that this couldn't go on much longer. A bit later, the aide called and said she was on her way; she had found the dry shampoo and wanted to wash his hair and she had been promising. And she did; she did it so gently and lovingly. When she was through, she leaned over and kissed him and said goodbye.

Late that afternoon, Tom was back, making some additional adjustments and checking on Charles' condition. He sat with us for a while and we talked. As he left that evening, Tom told me that he was sending a nurse in later that night to check on us. That evening, we celebrated Colin's birthday at dinner, waited, and watched.

A little before 11pm, the new nurse arrived. She and I went to turn him together and again his breathing changed; she asked me if I had seen him do that before. I hadn't. We turned him again and when she checked his blood pressure, it was very low … his breathing suddenly seemed to change again.

She looked at me and gave me the nod.

The others had been in the living room as she and I were turning him. I went into the living room and said, "This is it."

We all then gathered around the bed, Conor, Colin, Sean, Rob, Susan and myself, as we had done so many times in the past two weeks. I lay as close as I could to him … and within minutes he stopped breathing. He was gone. My Charles, the love of my life, was dead. I knew it and didn't want to know it. I ached for Conor and for Sean and Colin, who had just lost their father. I wanted to scream, and knew I wouldn't.

The hospice nurse, who was standing back in the kitchen said it was 11:58, and she quickly added that she could make it anytime we wanted, knowing that it was Colin's birthday. We all looked at him, and he said to keep it that time; it was OK.

I lay there with Charles for a few minutes; I am not sure whether anyone else was still in the room or not. And then it happened—the event that would change me forever.

As I lay there, I saw Charles' Spirit leave his body. At first, I thought I was hallucinating, but knew that I was not. I clearly saw it leave; it looked to me like "seeing your breath" when it is cold outside. I watched his spirit depart his body and rise into the air. I felt an instant, deep sense of peace and absolute certainty about what I had seen.

I will never have any doubts about the fact that the body and spirit do separate, and that experience made John's earlier words to me about the body not being the full person even more meaningful. The body, as he had said, was just a vessel. It wasn't so hard then, to talk about the funeral home coming to get Charles' body, because I knew that it was *only* his body; his spirit was someplace else.

In his dying, Charles had given me the greatest gift he could have. He had taught, by allowing me to see and to experience, that the ultimate force is love. It's the only thing that matters. When you die, you can't take your possessions with you, you can't take your body with you. After your spirit leaves, all that lasts is the love that you shared.

Chapter Twenty

• ◦ ● ◉ ● ● ◦ •

In my many years as a physician, I have had the privilege to attend many deaths. We would watch, and then there was "that moment", that moment when the heart stopped and the breathing stopped, and then we'd pronounce the person dead. It always struck me as odd because I always wondered, *isn't there something more?*

Clearly, there is more to life than the heartbeat and the breath. Or at least that is how it seems to me. What else happens at death? What really is the line between life and death? What is the substance that makes "life"? Is that the great mystery?

And now, I think I know that my intuition was right; it was more than the beating of the heart. It is the Spirit, the life force itself, that leaves the body when the heart stops beating and we stop breathing. A body without a spirit is a dead body; perhaps it is just that simple. And knowing that the spirit leaves the body made me know that it does, in fact, continue on after we are dead … how and where, I don't know. But I know that it does.

It was about 4 am when I finally went up the stairs to our bed. It was the first time I had been in our bed since hospice brought the hospital bed two weeks earlier. It seemed so empty. I couldn't really sleep, but I lay there for a couple of hours.

When the morning dawned, I got up and went outside. The forsythia was in bloom.

Epilogue

I f there is one universal truth, it is that we—each of us— must die. This is the only true constant, and it both defines us and changes us. Medicine (the medical profession) would do well to look at death less scientifically and more spiritually, allowing for the blending of the medicine and the mysticism, the science and the spiritual. Because, at some point, death eclipses all that we can bring to bear with science and medicine.

There are, it seems certain to me, worse things than dying. Being kept alive past the point where the balance is tipped towards non-ultimate survival, seems worse, at least to me. I suspect that there are many who share this perspective. Most people, when asked, say that they want to die at home. Why then, do so many die in hospitals, where death is experienced as a failure of the medical system rather than as the natural end of life, something not one of us can avoid? The ways, times and circumstances of death may all vary for us, but in the end, those of us who do not die a sudden death will have an experience of decline to our ultimate demise. And we can, in large part, determine the contours of that experience, if not the specifics along the way.

It is not about controlling the entire process, rather it is about making choices that reflect our own personal values and what is important to each of us in the process. When death becomes inevitable, we can choose for less intervention; to stay at home and receive such care as is practical and available. We might be able to choose specific aspects of our care, but perhaps not all. What is important is to be clear in stating our desires. And to do that, we need knowledge ... knowledge about possibilities, options, true prognosis, likely scenarios, etc. Only then can we decide which road we want to travel. The choice of road can be ours, but we cannot control every speed bump or intersection along the way.

Trust becomes a large part of the equation in the decision process. Trusting those providing the information, trusting those who will be providing our care, and trusting ourselves to make the best decisions at the time.

Death is the most common and least understood event in our lives, but we know that the dying process can be a powerful, beautiful and spiritually rich experience. My wish is that our medical profession will be able to move more in the direction of being able to support people in this process—understanding their decisions, providing them the most accurate information possible to make informed decisions about their lives and their deaths. Only then are we, as physicians, helping our patients heal by helping them die in the ways they choose, supporting them in the process and allowing for the mystical and spiritual aspects to be acknowledged.

I believe that both the dying process and the process of walking beside one who is dying can reflect back to us that which is true and important in our lives. The process can be the mirror into our own souls and offer us an opportunity to see and understand better what our priorities are.

Each of us will die one day. If our experience will ultimately be one of gradual decline, I challenge us to spend the time, have the difficult conversations, do the work that brings into the spotlight what is true and important to us. Share these desires with those who will be the ones to help us at the end of our lives.

It can make that final experience reflect our true selves and allow us to end our physical lives more in congruence with who we are, and have been, as people.